The
CHURCHILL
FACTORS

Creating Your Finest Hour

Larry Kryske

Trafford Publishing
Victoria, British Columbia, Canada

This book is intended to provide information concerning the subject matter covered. It is sold with the understanding that the publisher and author are not engaged in rendering legal, medical, psychological, or other professional services other than those which we are qualified to provide. If legal, medical, psychological, or other expert assistance is required, the services of competent professionals should be sought.

This book is not an attempt to be an exhaustive reference for all the subjects that lie between these covers. You are urged to read all available information on these subjects to give you the broadest and most complete discussion possible. Every effort has been made to make this book as accurate as possible. There may, however, be mistakes, both of a typographical nature and involving content. Accordingly, use this book with the proviso that it is a general guide and not the ultimate source of information on these subjects.

Since the purpose of this book is to educate and entertain, neither the author nor the publisher has any liability or responsibility to any person or entity with respect to any loss or damage caused, or alleged to be caused, directly or indirectly by the information contained in this book.

Cover Design: Debbie Romero
Cover: His Finest Hour, by Larry Kryske, 30 November 1987
Oil on canvas, 9 x 12" (22.9 x 30.5 cm)

Canadian Cataloguing in Publication Data

Kryske, Larry, 1949-
 The Churchill factors

 ISBN 1-55212-459-2

 1. Leadership. 2. Self-actualization (Psychology) 3. Churchill,
Winston S. (Winston Spencer), 1874-1965. I. Title.
BF637.L4K79 2000   158'.4   C00-911064-X

TRAFFORD

This book was published *on-demand* in cooperation with Trafford Publishing.
On-demand publishing is a unique process and service of making a book available for retail sale to the public taking advantage of on-demand manufacturing and Internet marketing.
On-demand publishing includes promotions, retail sales, manufacturing, order fulfilment, accounting and collecting royalties on behalf of the author.

Suite 6E, 2333 Government St., Victoria, B.C. V8T 4P4, CANADA

Phone	250-383-6864	Toll-free	1-888-232-4444 (Canada & US)
Fax	250-383-6804	E-mail	sales@trafford.com
Web site	www.trafford.com	TRAFFORD PUBLISHING IS A DIVISION OF TRAFFORD HOLDINGS LTD.	
Trafford Catalogue #00-0124		www.trafford.com/robots/00-0124.html	

10   9   8   7   6   5   4   3   2   1

Dedicated to:

**My parents, Leon & Annette,
who gave me life,**

**and my wife, Naomi,
who gave me back my life.**

*"You cannot teach a man anything. You
can only help him to find it within himself."*
Galileo

Table of Contents

PART • FOUR
The Landscape of Leadership

PART • FIVE
Mobilizing the English Language

PART • SIX
Applying the Churchill Factors

APPENDICES

Preface

On Sunday, January 24, 1965, a fifteen-year-old high school student sat in his father's chair in their suburban Los Angeles home reading the newspaper. He was also listening to the radio. The 1:00 PM news opened with the announcement of the passing of Sir Winston Churchill. As he listened to the news story, the boy experienced a sense of sadness. This confused him since he did not really know much about the great man. A question formed in the boy's mind: "Who was Winston Churchill?"

As the boy discovered, Churchill had lived a long life, and so the boy's interest occupied him longer than he expected.

Where did this curiosity about Churchill lead? The student who "discovered" Churchill later served as a career naval officer, a private school administrator, and a professional speaker and seminar leader. He published articles about Winston Churchill, took up oil painting largely because of Churchill's example, gave hundreds of speeches about Churchill nationwide, served a term on the Board of Directors of the International Churchill

Society, and met (and later married) the woman of his dreams at a Churchill Society convention. They became, in Churchill's words, another "English-speaking union"!

January 24, 1965, may have been Sir Winston Churchill's final hour, but for me—the student—it was the birth of a life-long study of Churchill and of ways to share his leadership wisdom to help others attain their finest hour.

Larry Kryske
June 18, 2000

"I expect the Battle of Britain is about to begin. Upon this battle depends the survival of Christian civilization. Upon it depends our own British life, and the long continuity of our institutions and our Empire. The whole fury and might of the enemy must very soon be turned on us. Hitler knows that he will have to break us in this island or lose the war. If we can stand up to him, all Europe may be free and the life of the world may move forward into broad, sunlit uplands. But if we fail, then the whole world, including the United States, including all that we have known and cared for, will sink into the abyss of a new Dark Age made more sinister, and perhaps more protracted, by the lights of perverted science. Let us there brace ourselves to our duties, and so bear ourselves that, if the British Empire and its Commonwealth last for a thousand years, men will still say, 'This was their finest hour.'"

Winston Churchill
June 18, 1940

Introduction

This book can change your life! If you are looking for a way to get off the treadmill of frustration and despair and start living the life of your dreams, you have come to the right place. The message of hope contained in this book can propel you toward your dreams. It can help you create *your* finest hour.

The Churchill Factors is for the person who is pressed for time. You will not have to wade through laundry lists of leadership principles that are hard to remember. Instead, you will discover what really matters most about personal leadership and achieving your dreams. By keeping the ideas simple, practical, and timely, you will be able to apply these concepts right away.

This book uses Winston Churchill as a role model. Unlike most of the books about Churchill, this one will not bombard you with a large number of facts, figures, or analyses of his life. That is the job for biographers and historians. *The Churchill Factors* can more accurately be called "applied Churchill." You will learn about Churchill's best practices involving leadership as well as his proven strategies for success.

> ***"Knowing is not enough; we must apply.***
> ***Willing is not enough; we must do."***
> **Goethe**

The real value of history is not the knowledge itself, but rather the application of the knowledge to live a more productive and fulfilling life. The late Russell Kelfer perhaps said it best when he observed, "When knowledge becomes personal, we have understanding. Applying this understanding yields wisdom." Thus, the goal of this book is not to give you knowledge about Churchill, but rather his understanding of life that he distilled into wisdom.

In his celebrated 1923 book, *The Art Spirit*, artist Robert Henri observed, "Simplicity is the soul of art." This belief can equally be applied to our lives. Simplicity is the soul of life! This does not imply that life is simple. Science and other disciplines have brought us an overabundance of information about every subject, including leadership and Churchill. Life is indeed complex, but if we can help other people to understand, and then apply, what they have learned, they will be able to benefit from this new understanding.

Many of today's historians seem preoccupied with denigrating the decisions and character of men like

Churchill. It is truly unfortunate that these learned writers second-guess decisions made by others in the heat of battle and with imperfect knowledge while they have abundant, detailed information gleaned years after the events from all parties involved. These 20/20 hindsight commentators should be more humble! Therefore, three quotations will serve as our guide.

"Many of those who write about history like to seem wiser than those who made history."
David Howarth

"Both Lincoln and Churchill have not lacked their critics; the reputations of both seem likely to endure."
Maxwell Schoenfeld

"Criticism is easy; achievement is more difficult."
Winston Churchill

Look in any bookstore and you'll find shelves devoted to every facet of leadership. (That's because leadership is one of those topics that we recognize as vitally important to our survival, both in business and in our personal lives.) We can learn the leadership secrets of everyone from Attila the Hun to Abraham Lincoln to Captain Kirk of "Star Trek." We can find books about leadership that is invented, reinvented, visionary, strategic, servant, maximized, charismatic, innovative, intuitive, breakthrough, and enlightened. We can also have our leadership by the numbers—the seven habits, the fourteen points, the twenty-one irrefutable laws, or the hundred-and-one stories.

Before I go any further, do not misread my intentions. I firmly believe that every book on leadership has some value. In addition, I have personally benefited from reading, absorbing, and applying the nuggets found in the works of contemporary and classical thinkers.

I seek, however, to simplify leadership in much the same way a cartoonist simplifies the face and body of a noteworthy political figure. If you look at the work of some of the best cartoonists, you'll notice that they have captured the essence of their subject with just a few strategically-drawn lines. They could have reproduced their subject in faithful photographic detail. Instead, they portrayed only those most significant features that reminded the reader of the person.

> *"All the great things are simple,*
> *and many can be expressed in a single word:*
> *freedom; justice; honor; duty; mercy; hope."*
> **Winston Churchill**

Simplifying a subject like leadership means capturing its essence with as few brushstrokes as possible. Each chapter in *The Churchill Factors* will give you tools you can use immediately. You won't have to master a great list of principles before you can apply them to the task at hand. Just as a hammer or screwdriver is a simple tool, the simple leadership insights in this book will let you get to work on your professional or personal life right away.

This book is intended for ALL people. There are leadership strengths and talents in every one of us! Executives, employees, homemakers, students—all can benefit from a methodology that can help us lead a richer, fuller, more productive life. If we can lead more complete lives at home, our time at work will be more productive. Similarly, if work becomes more satisfying, our life at home will be smoother. Thus, our professional and personal lives are directly related to each other. If one suffers, the other will ultimately suffer.

> *"The true task of leadership is not to put greatness into humanity, but to elicit it, since the greatness is already there."*
> **John Buchan**

The world cries out for leaders. Where have all the leaders gone? The answer is: they're still here! Leadership potential resides in every one of us—every man, every woman, and every child. The potential is there, but sometimes it is dormant, waiting for that critical moment of decision or crisis. The good news is that by using a simple formula for success, everyone can harness the power of leadership to create his or her finest hour.

PART ● ONE

Changing
Your Destiny

1

Your Finest Hour

There is a special time in each person's life when all of his or her past preparations become perfectly aligned with some significant opportunity. When a person steps forward and seizes that opportunity, he fulfills his destiny. That is his finest hour!

Not long after Winston Churchill became Prime Minister on May 10, 1940, he was called upon to exercise decision-making powers that would prove critical to the survival of Britain, Western Europe, and the free world. History has reported that his bold stand for freedom made him the man for that moment. He was one of those precious few to be called an indispensable man. Churchill felt as if he were "walking with Destiny and all [his] past life had been but a preparation for this trial." This historical milestone became his finest hour.

By studying the life of Churchill, we can observe that there were actually several times when he was the man of the hour. These significant events in history were not the result of luck or "happy accidents" or wishful thinking. They were the culmination of years of preparation. Churchill thoroughly and painstakingly prepared himself by continuously improving his communications skills, his knowledge of world affairs, and his understanding of human nature.

In addition, Churchill prepared himself by taking on challenging tasks. He chose to take a stand for certain points of view knowing that some people would not just disagree with him, but would vilify him in the most cruel ways. For example, his almost singular stand against Hitler initially earned him the criticism and ridicule of the government, the press, and the man on the street.

Furthermore, Churchill could not have arrived on the world scene in 1940 ready to play his part without first having been involved in years of lesser struggles, trials, and tests. Early in his political career, Churchill believed that he had a special role to play in the life of his country. More than three decades before he became Prime Minister, he said, "We are all worms. But I do believe I am a glow worm." He knew that he had to prepare himself to be ready for the time destiny would call to him.

All of us have the ability to create our finest hour. We cannot know specifically, however, how we will be called upon to play our part. Perhaps it will involve our families or friends. Perhaps it will concern our careers, professions, or workplaces. Perhaps it will involve some service to our country or our church. Perhaps it will be a matter of conscience for which we will take a stand. Our finest hour will occur when our years of preparation meet some crucial opportunity.

FINEST HOUR = PREPARATION + OPPORTUNITY

To create our finest hour means living our lives on purpose. Rather than coasting through life on cruise control, we must be conscious of the world about us and take responsibility for our actions. How easy it is to see but not observe, to hear but not listen! We can choose to let others decide how we live our lives or we can choose to decide for ourselves.

There is no age barrier concerning your ability to create your finest hour. Whether you are 20 or 70, there are countless examples of people who chose to get off the treadmill of life and walk with purpose toward their finest hour.

"Because of Churchill's greatness, people lost what they most needed losing—their cynicism and feelings of tentativeness and panic in the face of national and personal danger. It was not Churchill's rhetoric alone that enabled them to do this. It was the recognition he gave them that history was what men made it."
Norman Cousins

All of us must use the special gifts, talents, skills, and abilities that we have been given. Combining these with what we have learned from our successes and setbacks uniquely qualifies us to meet the challenges that significant opportunities bring. By refocusing our efforts in a structured way, we can get more of the things we want to be, do, or have in this life. We do this by making small "course corrections" to our behaviors based on new information we learn. Big surprises can come from small packages!

"A mighty flame followeth a tiny spark."
Dante

The power of small changes is best illustrated by a phenomenon called the "butterfly effect." Scientists have theorized that a butterfly flapping its wings could cause a disturbance to the air. This disturbance could create an amplified chain reaction across the entire atmosphere. Ultimately, this reaction could produce a hurricane. (A meteorologist first suggested this possibility, using a seagull's wings, as an application of Nobel Laureate Konrad Lorentz's principle, "The Sensitive Dependence on Initial Conditions.")

Do you believe the "butterfly effect"? Let me share with you a compelling example. A long time ago there lived a man in his early thirties. Thirty-something! He never went to college. He never raised a family. He never had a home of his own. He never wrote a book. He never received any special honors or recognitions. He never held any political office. During the three years he worked at his calling, he never traveled more than 120 miles from where he was born. He coached and mentored twelve friends, and eleven remained faithful to him. Two thousand years later, he has over a billion followers! This is the "butterfly effect"!

Although this may be the ultimate example of the "butterfly effect," the important point is that a small change in one area of your life can create a profound difference in your destiny! The small changes you make in your life day by day will prepare you for the time when a significant opportunity calls to you.

"The secret of success
is consistency of purpose."
Benjamin Disraeli

There is a simple methodology for success that can help all of us prepare for our finest hour. We can live our lives with intention and know that when the opportunities present themselves, we will be ready. Then it will be our finest hour!

2

An Anchor of Hope

Hope makes the sun rise for most of us each day. We all have a desire that our expectations will somehow be fulfilled. Hope gives us a reason to press on with life. Hope, then, is one of those singular human qualities that allows us to continue in the face of hardships, obstacles, and criticisms.

"The function of a leader is to keep hope alive."
John W. Gardner

Is it possible to give some certainty to the hopes we have in life? Can hope be transformed from a random event into something that can be specifically sought and achieved? The power of harnessing hope is simpler than you may think.

Before we discuss how to "create" hope, we must first prune back some of the dead branches that prevent our tree of life from fully blossoming in the sunlight of new opportunities. Most people carry a great deal of emotional baggage with them from place to place, job to job, and relationship to relationship. This baggage darkens our lives rather than quickening our spirits. We expend a great deal of emotional energy being angry, resentful, or sorrowful. This negative energy robs our vitality and strength. In fact, it literally saps the life from our lives.

People also bring another interesting mindset with them. They believe that things will magically get better in their "next life." What is that "next life"? It is the one that starts when the kids go to school or when they finally finish college. It is when you land that new job or when you finally retire. It is a moving target: like a mirage, it disappears just before you reach it.

So how do we prune back the dead growth of emotional baggage? It starts with a basic understanding of who we are. What separates us from other animals? We are blessed with free will. We have choice. Rather than act on the basis of instinct, we can act based on the result of thoughts. Thoughts are our most powerful tool, but they can also be our most destructive weapon.

> ## *"Don't let poverty of circumstance result in poverty of the spirit."*
> **Naomi Kryske**

We can choose our response to what happens. We can choose to be a winner or a loser. We can choose to be a victor or a victim. We can look at some event and say, "It's not enough," or we can report, "It's plenty for me."

We can let our choices color our world in darkness or we can let the light shine through.

The power of our choice is limited only by our imagination and our will. Sir Walter Scott once spoke of "the will to do and the soul to dare." We take responsibility for our lives by taking responsibility for our responses to what happens in our lives. Once we do this, then we can begin to harness hope and live our dreams.

"Where there is hope in the future,
there's power in the present."
Les Brown

Over two thousand years ago, men in the Holy Land used the anchor as a symbol of hope. Today we can harness the power of hope by anchoring ourselves in proven leadership techniques. Thus, with hope and personal leadership we can create our finest hour!

3

Putting the Past
in the Past

Each of us was created by God to be a masterpiece. Each of us possesses all the innate talents to lead a joyful, productive, successful life. Do you believe that? Most of us have trouble thinking that we already have the talents to be successful.

We all can choose our responses to what happens to us. We all possess imagination and the ability to persevere. Regardless of the differences in our educational backgrounds, professional experiences, and personal histories, we have inner strengths that, if used, can ensure our survival. These strengths are derived from our thoughts. When our thoughts become actions, we can create the kind of lives we desire.

Life is about discovering these inner strengths. Each of us is blessed with certain gifts and talents. For example, some of us prefer to deal with people, others with things, and still others with information. Some people are decisive and task oriented. Others may have the ability to encourage and inspire people. Some people may be sensitive to the needs of others. And some may be analytical and detail oriented. We need to discover our strengths and then develop strategies to put them to use.

Life is also about claiming those special gifts and talents that only you possess and generously sharing them with the other people on this planet. This is what Albert Schweitzer meant when he said we were to "invest our humanity."

How can one person have an impact on humanity? Try the old-fashioned way, by influencing one person at a time. Start with your immediate family or perhaps with your co-workers or friends. Sharing your time and talents with them can enrich their lives and have an indelible effect on them. Giving people hope is a precious gift.

On the other hand, it is truly sad when a person gives up hope. When did you lose the exuberance of your childhood? When did you squelch the spontaneity of your teenage years? When did you discard the drive and ambition of your 20's, 30's, or 40's? When did you stop pursuing your dreams?

So how does a person shed the emotional baggage and begin the process of harnessing hope? Should we start in the past? Some believe that the past is the best predictor of the future. Others may agree with George Santayana, who said, "Those who fail to learn from history are doomed to relive it." These mindsets, however, can prevent us from ever escaping the closed world of our past.

"The past is a place of reference, not a place of residence."
Willie Jolley

We must learn from the past but not be controlled by it. We need to move on. Remember, we have free will or choice. Choice means our future does not have to come from our past. This bears repeating: choice means our future does not have to come from our past! The good news is that we can blaze a new trail.

The key, then, is to put the past in the past. First, think about this: can you undo something that has already occurred in the past? Does worrying about it ever change what happened? Now consider this: would you ever drive your car down the freeway by looking only through your rearview mirror? Of course not! But isn't this exactly what many of us do with our lives? We try to move forward while looking back.

To put the past in the past, you must look to something in the present. For example, if you harbor ill feelings about what another person did to you in the past, then forgiveness may be a way to cast off this needless emotional baggage. Forgiveness, therefore, is something we do for ourselves, not for the other person.

Forgiveness does not mean that we condone or approve of what happened. Forgiveness means letting go. We are not going to dwell on the issue or concern. Forgiveness allows us to let out a sigh of relief and stop expending emotional energy that keeps us from moving forward with our lives.

Withdraw your emotional investment from those destructive, toxic, or negative events in your past. Think about this: what does it cost to you to keep feelings of anger, frustration, or despair about something that has already occurred? The energy expended to keep those old hurts alive prevents you from making progress in your life.

"I have learnt through bitter experience the one supreme lesson: to conserve my anger, and as heat conserved is transmuted into energy, even so our anger controlled can be transmuted into a power which can move the world."
Mahatma Gandhi

The difficulty we have with putting the past in the past is directly proportional to our emotional investment. The greater the feelings involved, the more difficult it will be to get over the event. The principle, however, is the same. The past is—past! It's over, it's lost to us. Free will allows us to choose to accept it as a loss, rather than being angry or regretful. It is far better to be sad than mad—because sadness, or grief, is a healing process. It is a healthy way of dealing with unresolved feelings about the past. Healing will allow us to move forward.

Grief over people, jobs, or homes, for example, becomes a way of putting the past in the past. Grief is like a river that winds back and forth, east and west, while flowing south to the sea. At the headwaters of grief lie shock, denial, or disbelief at what happened. As the river flows south, strong emotions may cause the water to boil explosively against the rocks and shore. Emotions like depression, isolation, panic, fear, guilt, anger, or resentment are common. As some of the river's energy is lost, a period of bargaining occurs in which the river looks for the path of least resistance. Finally the river can no longer avoid running to the sea and accepts the course that nature has set for her.

We grieve for loved ones who have passed away or for relationships that have gone astray. We grieve for the loss of a job or for friends we leave behind when we move. We also grieve when we discover how our old ways have prevented us from saying or doing the things we felt to those we love. We grieve when we make those big insights and learn the cost to us and others of our behavior. Grieving is a natural process that can help us to put the past in the past.

Another way to put the past in the past is to live in the present. This does not mean living *for* the present. Rather, it is the realization that the present is the only time domain where we have some influence or control. We can't change the past, and we can't guarantee the future. Thus, we need to give greater emphasis to the present.

> *"We can only pay our debt to the past by putting the future in the debt to ourselves."*
> **John Buchan**

We live in the present by living one day at a time. Once again, this does not mean we can't learn from the past or plan for the future. However, when we clear our minds of thoughts that clutter it—old, limiting thoughts—we make room for new and empowering thoughts.

Still another way to put the past in the past is by the way we speak to ourselves, our self-talk. We can choose an explanation about what happened that encourages or empowers us as opposed to one that is negative or discouraging. By focusing on the positive, we are creating an opening for the possibility of a positive outcome. Our brain's function is to ensure our survival. To do this, the brain wants to make us "right." We only get what we expect. A positive expectation will cause our brain to select—from those millions of bits of data that bombard our senses—only those that will fulfill our expectation. Thus, if we want a great day, we must precondition our brain by telling it that we will have a great day.

Don't let your past hold back your future! Today is a new day! Exercise your power of choice!

"A ship doesn't sail with yesterday's wind."
Louis L'Amour

Let's give ourselves permission to start again, wherever we are. Like the artist, we can begin with a clean, unpainted canvas and rediscover the masterpiece that lies within us.

Churchill recognized the importance of taking action. During the Second World War, he placed small red labels with the words "Action This Day" on the instructions and decision papers he sent to his staff. This helped create a sense of urgency that what the staff was doing was vitally important to the war effort. We, too, must have a sense of urgency. Each day we must take some actions toward our dreams if we are to create our finest hour.

ACTION THIS DAY

1. What baggage are you carrying that is causing you to expend emotional energy? What is this baggage preventing (or interfering with) you from being or doing?

2. What words do you use in your self-talk to describe this baggage?

3. Can you look at the baggage from a different, more empowering viewpoint? If so, what words can you use to describe it?

4. Is there someone in your life that you need to forgive, so you can move on with what's important to you?

5. What is the cost to you and your life by not forgiving this person(s)?

6. What will be the benefits of forgiving this person(s)? To what will you now be able to devote more of your time?

4

The Churchill Factors

Let's start with a true story about a young boy. His family was fairly well to do, actually wealthy by upper middle class standards. He lived in a fine home, wore nice clothes, and had an abundance of toys. So far, it seems he had a great deal going for him, but read on.

This boy was not particularly good looking or athletic. Rather, he was pudgy and somewhat ungainly. Physically he was frail, and he was often sick. He spoke with a lisp. He did poorly in school, and his teachers thought he was a troublemaker. Worse yet, the boy's parents rarely found time to be with him. If they loved him, they certainly did not show it. Thus at the start of his young life, he lacked two of the three things children need most: parental love and encouragement. (He did have security.)

This boy's future did not look very promising. He seemed to have very little going for him, except for one thing. Inside his head, he had a very different picture of

himself. He didn't see himself in terms of all his
negatives. Rather, he saw himself taking bold, dynamic
actions. He wasn't being an awkward, restless,
troublesome child. Instead, he was commanding warriors
in desperate battles. He wasn't stuttering when he spoke.
Rather, he was giving eloquent speeches to thrilled
audiences. You see, this boy had a vision of himself!

Isn't that amazing? That's what a vision can do. It
can transform a person into a new person! Do you still
have a vision of yourself?

"The ancestor of every action is a thought."
Ralph Waldo Emerson

Now let me share with you a story about a prisoner of
war, a POW. After he was captured, he was taken to a
POW camp over 300 miles from the nearest friendly
lines. Several of the other prisoners in the camp spoke
about escaping, but most were too afraid to break free.
The POW in our story felt differently about his captivity.

Unlike his fellow prisoners, this POW just *had* to
escape. It didn't matter that he didn't speak any of the
native languages. It didn't matter that he didn't know the
local terrain. It didn't matter that he was not equipped to
survive in the wilderness that lay between the POW camp
and friendly lines. It didn't matter that there probably
wouldn't be anyone sympathetic to him inside enemy
territory. What *did* matter was his vision of freedom. The
POW had a vision of freedom that gave him the courage
to act.

If this POW had carefully assessed his situation and considered all the risks, he probably would not have taken that first step toward escaping. But he did take that first step, and his escape was successful. What did it take for the POW to step outside his personal comfort zone and risk everything? It took courage.

You are the only one who can to decide to escape from your past into your future. How would your life be transformed if you stepped outside your personal comfort zone?

"Character is far more important than intellect in making a man a good citizen or successful at his calling—meaning by character not only such qualities as honesty and truthfulness, but courage, perseverance and self-reliance."
Theodore Roosevelt

Finally, let's consider a third story, this time about a public servant. All he ever wanted to do was to serve his country, either in war or in peace. He thought a war was coming, but no one believed him. At this critical point in his life he had no official power base, because he no longer had a position in the government. Still, this public servant felt sure war was coming. He just could not sit back and do nothing. So what did he do?

He gathered his own intelligence about the military and political situation facing his country. He asked probing questions. He asked still more questions. He listened carefully and thought about what he learned. He believed that his country was in terrible danger. And then he spoke. He spoke through public speeches. He spoke through newspaper and magazine articles. He spoke through radio broadcasts and books.

Did it make a difference? No, not at first. People laughed. So what did he do? He spoke. He spoke to public audiences, large and small. He spoke to the press. He spoke by whatever means he could find.

They laughed; they ridiculed him; they said he was crazy. So what did he do? He spoke! He spoke for almost ten long years. He used every avenue he could to warn his countrymen. It took almost a decade before they began to listen.

What did it take for him to persevere in the face of such opposition? It took determination. It took repeating the same action, over and over again. It took the will to never give in!

What would be the impact on your life if you were able to follow through with your vision until you ultimately achieved it?

"You will make many journeys.
Always keep in mind your destination
or you may never get there."
Mahatma Gandhi

Vision, **courage**, and **determination** are the three key factors a person needs to create his or her finest hour. In fact, I call them the Churchill Factors.

The Churchill Factors:

VISION
COURAGE
DETERMINATION

Most people remember Winston Churchill for his dynamic leadership as Prime Minister of Great Britain during the Second World War. His famous "V" for victory, his ever-present cigar, and his defiant speeches were his trademarks.

Winston Churchill, however, was much more. He was one of the truly great renaissance men of all time. He was a statesman and warrior, an administrator and historian, an orator and artist, as well as a bricklayer and journalist. Churchill did not just participate in these activities, but rather he demonstrated mastery of these diverse fields. This mastery gave him a stature equaled by few in the twentieth century.

The three stories presented earlier were about his life. The boy with the vision of himself that no one else had—that was Winston Churchill. The POW with the courage to escape—that was Winston Churchill. The speaker who wouldn't give up—that, too, was Winston Churchill. Despite all his successes, his road to greatness was neither straight nor smooth! Churchill had the ability to turn adversity into advantage.

Churchill found relief from the demands of his work in oil painting. He once said he preferred to paint landscapes, since "trees didn't complain when he failed to do them justice." He managed to complete over six hundred oil paintings, sandwiched among his other significant career achievements. His books numbered over fifty large volumes. He authored over a thousand magazine and newspaper articles. He gave thousands of speeches. How many words was that? Over thirty million! He was determined!

He served sixty years in Parliament, held almost every cabinet post in the British government, and was the Prime Minister twice—the first time when he was 65 (that's when most people retire), and the second time when he was 76. And as we know, he also spent some time out of office.

> ### "I have nothing to offer but blood, toil, tears, and sweat."
> **Winston Churchill**

In almost every phase of his ninety-year life, Churchill's use of vision, courage, and determination was readily apparent. This remarkable man attracted both devoted champions and persistent detractors. Few people have been neutral about him, but Churchill's successes speak for themselves. His incredible power of concentration and ability to focus intently helped him to use his time effectively. His impressive output of written and spoken words, while at the same time being fully involved in demanding leadership positions, speaks to his productivity.

> *"To pursue mental operations to any depth, a person has to learn to concentrate attention. Without focus, consciousness is in a state of chaos."*
> **Mihaly Csikszentmihalyi**

Churchill's tenacious bulldog persistence was legendary. He overcame great personal and political obstacles numerous times in his life. Whether the villains were his lisp, his frail childhood body, the absence of parental love, his lack of a formal college education, his political defeats, his war of survival against dictators, his loss of a child, or his inner battles with depression, he became a symbol of raw personal courage.

> *"I am certainly not one of those who need to be prodded. In fact, if anything, I am the prod."*
> **Winston Churchill**

Churchill was also a matchless innovator and a champion of continuous innovation. Throughout his life, he proved that he was a man well ahead of his time. He not only seized the opportunities presented by a paradigm shift but became quite a paradigm shifter himself. He devised tactical and strategic innovations with equal aplomb. The blinders that shield a person's receptivity to new ideas must have been wide open for Churchill. His legacy involving the tank, naval aviation, prison reform, and pension plans, for example, ought to shine as clearly as his brilliant strategic ideas during both World Wars I and II. Only Churchill, a leading defender of the moribund British Empire, could challenge new generations with, "the empires of the future are the empires of the mind."

"Churchill knew the difference between what is transient and what is timeless."
Dean Pope

Churchill was criticized by his contemporaries for being an intuitive decision maker. His prophecies of the two world wars and the Cold War were appreciated mostly in hindsight. Churchill, however, was not just a visionary or prophet. There is a distinction between perceiving the future and making it happen. The key to his intuitive powers came from the interaction of his artistic right brain with his analytical left brain.

Churchill, in effect, was more of a whole brain thinker. Perhaps his right brain accomplishments enabled him to bring more of his brain power into focus. Bold oil paintings, the poetic meter to his written works, and the drama of his speeches say much about his right brain development.

Three other elements contributed to his intuitive success. First, Churchill was a non-linear thinker. That is to say, the cause and effect of his decision-making process appeared to be unrelated. On the contrary, he was more in tune with the real world, which is also non-linear. Second, he was blessed with a phenomenal memory that helped him retain an extensive historical data base. Third, his keen awareness of human nature helped him understand the motivations of others and anticipate their actions. All these characteristics synergized with his other right brain gifts, allowing Churchill the ability to see beyond the horizon.

Churchill's superior communication skills as a writer, orator, and artist, made him a powerful role model. His eloquence, energy, emotion, and wit were only exceeded by his humanity. His magnanimous win-win attitude toward vanquished foes was demonstrated countless times during his long political career. He once noted, "Generosity is always wise."

"...human beings are not dominated by material things, but by ideas for which they are willing to give their lives or their life's work."
Winston Churchill

Whether he was embracing new technology, displaying a sensitivity to diplomatic negotiations, or motivating a nation gripped by despair and defeat, Churchill was a resilient man of uncommon optimism, enthusiasm, generosity, compassion, and honor. His greatest legacy, however, will not be his considerable intellectual achievements, nor his brilliant social and military innovations, nor his brave deeds. His indelible mark on history will rest on his life-long example as a leader.

5

How to Use This Book

Churchill once observed, "The human story does not unfold like a mathematical calculation." That's because people are different. They see the world differently. They have different informational needs. They possess different degrees of willingness to take risks. This can and does create misunderstandings if, for example, the author is a "big picture" person and the reader is detail oriented. In books of this nature, the "one size fits all" approach may not be completely helpful.

In order to accommodate the different behavioral preferences of people, I have tailored portions of this book to each basic type or style of person. Each designated section has been written from the viewpoint and in language most appropriate for that style. In addition, the questions at the ends of the chapters have been directed toward that particular style.

In our world, we must interact with all kinds of people, people of every behavioral preference. If we are to learn how to understand, value, and appreciate others, we must know more about the people who are different from us. This book will help us understand better our co-workers, bosses, and employees, as well as family and friends.

"O wad some pow'r the giftie gie us,
To see oursels as ithers see us!"
Robert Burns

Imagine you hear someone knocking at your door. As you open the door, there facing you is: you! Would you like the person you see facing you? Would he or she be your friend? Would you hire that person to work for you? The process of understanding others begins with first understanding yourself.

Let's take a short course on what it means to be a human. Presented in layman's terms, it is intended to simplify concepts and help us understand some of the subtleties involving personality and behavior.

Each person is born with certain genetic traits inherited from his parents. These define who we are: what color hair we have, how tall we are, etc. For all practical purposes, we can consider these genetic traits essentially unchangeable. When the newborn, the toddler, and later the child, interact with his or her environment (people, places, events, etc.), a core personality develops. The young person has little or no influence on how this personality is scripted for him. By the time a person reaches early teens, the personality development process is essentially complete. (It may have been completed much earlier.)

Core personality, for the most part, is also not easily altered. Life-changing events, trauma, therapy, and other factors can help a person to change his core personality. It is also difficult to discern a person's core personality. We usually cannot tell just by looking at a person if he prefers to work with people, things, or information. Similarly, we cannot readily discern many of the other aspects of core personality.

When a person's core personality interacts with the environment, the responses produce thoughts (beliefs, attitudes, values, motivations, etc.). These thoughts cause us to have certain emotional responses or feelings (fear, love, happiness, anger, etc.) that in turn result in certain actions or behaviors.

Behaviors are observable. We can see them in others as well as be conscious of our own behaviors. Behaviors are also changeable, that is, a person can adapt to different situations with different behaviors. A person who is cold and reserved in one situation can be warm and outgoing in another.

Thus, in dealing with people, we must deal with behaviors instead of core personality, since we can observe behaviors. More often then not, when someone says a person's "personality" is cheerful, they are probably referring to behavior, not core personality.

There are four basic behavioral preferences or dimensions. Each of us is a combination of all four. Each of us tends to favor one or more of these dimensions.

Since the purpose here is to give the reader enough background to use this book effectively, I am greatly simplifying both the identification and the nature of each behavior.

"Human beings and human societies are not structures that are built or machines that are forged. They are plants that grow and must be tended as such. Life is a test and this world a place of trial. Always the problems, or it may be the same problem, will be presented to every generation in different forms."
Winston Churchill

We will look at each of the four behavioral styles. In this case, the word "styles" means tendencies, preferences, or dimensions of behavior. Remember, each of us possesses each of the four styles, but at least one may be more prominent for us.

Before we go any further, please pay close attention to the following observation. No one style is better than the others. No one style is found to a greater extent in leaders, creative people, CEOs, PhDs, or other successful people. Did you get that? There is no such thing as one best style! Let me repeat that for emphasis. **There is NO best or preferred style!** Each of us has some of each of the four styles in us. We tend to use some of the styles more than others, but we can learn to use any of the styles to help us in a particular situation.

Let's now look briefly at each of the styles.

DRIVERS

People who exhibit the first behavioral style we will discuss can be called **Drivers**. These are fast-paced individuals who are mission driven. They want to get the job done. They are direct, "bottom line" people. Drivers are:

- **Results or task oriented**
- **Take-charge individuals**
- **Risk takers**
- **Confident**
- **Energized by challenges and change**
- **Decisive**

Drivers are results-oriented people who can work well independently. They can be strong willed and competitive. They boldly (and sometimes loudly) shape their environment. Their greatest need is to control their environment and thus, their greatest fear is losing control of a situation.

Drivers can have some limiting traits. They may be too direct in their dealings with others. This bluntness is the result of their desire to get the job done first. Drivers think about mission first and people second, hence, they may come across as insensitive or uncaring. In their desire to gain results, they may become impatient, aggressive, and demanding. They tend to be poor listeners and too sparing in the giving of compliments.

Drivers fill a vital need in both professional and personal kinds of venues. These forceful, decisive, results-oriented people deal extremely well with both challenges and change. They are quick-minded decision makers based on their perception of the big picture and the bottom line.

INFLUENCERS

People who exhibit the second behavioral style we will study can be called **Influencers**. These fast-paced individuals are people oriented. Influencers are:

- **Good communicators**
- **Enthusiastic**
- **Socially outgoing**
- **Persuasive**
- **Fun loving**
- **Optimistic**

Influencers can be extremely charming, sociable individuals who are talkative, animated, emotional, and stimulating. They can be positive, inspiring, and powerful communicators. They bring an element of fun to an organization. They tell jokes and keep the atmosphere light.

Since their greatest need is the approval of other people, Influencers fear social rejection or loss of influence. These friendly, outgoing people do not like working alone or having to deal with many details.

Influencers can have some limiting traits. They may come across as too talkative, unrealistic, disorganized, emotional, manipulative, and vain. In their dealings with others, they may exaggerate, become pushy, and ignore details. Influencers sometimes overcompliment people, thus reducing the value of the acknowledgement they give to others.

Influencers are the cheerleaders in professional and personal venues. They bring optimism and excitement into our lives. Their keen understanding of human nature means that they tend to be impulsive decision makers relying on their gut feel for a situation.

SUPPORTERS

People who exhibit the third behavioral style we will examine can be called **Supporters**. These people-oriented individuals have a more reserved pace of activity. Supporters are:

- **Methodical and meticulous**
- **Patient and calm**
- **Loyal**
- **Good team players**
- **Empathic listeners**
- **Understanding and sympathetic**

Supporters are warm, relational people who express sincere appreciation of others. They see their role as supporting, cooperating, nurturing, and helping others. They make great team players and can be relied upon to complete an assignment.

Supporters like to maintain a certain stability in their lives. They tend to fear change, unpredictability, and loss of stability. Conflicts also upset them.

They can have some limiting traits. As they strive to maintain the status quo, they may become indecisive and over-accommodating. They may be highly sensitive, easily manipulated by others, and resistant to change. They need sufficient time to adapt to change, and they need to feel appreciated by others.

Supporters are compassionate, understanding people. Their easy, calming, encouraging demeanor brings stability and harmony to professional and personal venues. They possess exceptional listening abilities. They are trusting of others and arrive at decisions based on their generous acceptance of other people.

CONCEPTUALIZERS

People who exhibit the fourth behavioral style we will cover are called **Conceptualizers**. These mission-oriented people also prefer a more reserved pace of activity. Conceptualizers are:

- **Detail oriented**
- **Analytical**
- **Tactful or diplomatic**
- **Orderly and precise**
- **Logical**
- **Independent**

Conceptualizers strive for accuracy and quality in their environments by remaining within established rules, regulations, and procedures. They approach situations cautiously and require adequate time to analyze the pros and cons of a situation.

Since Conceptualizers have high personal standards of accuracy, they fear being criticized for the quality of their work. They also dislike disorganized or ambiguous explanations as well as situations that appear irrational or emotionally out of control.

They can have some limiting traits. They may become overly critical and judgmental of themselves and others. Conceptualizers tend to worry too much about what could happen and may become suspicious. Since they prefer to work independently, they may become loners and not participate on a team. Their perfectionism may prevent them from taking needed risks and reaching decisions.

Conceptualizers are reflective, thoughtful individuals who often become the honest brokers in professional and personal venues. They consider the pros and cons of an activity. Their high standards and attention to detail ensure that things are being done according to established rules and with the appropriate resources.

Before we continue, please take the following short quiz concerning the four styles:

1. Which behavioral style is best?
❏ **Drivers**
❏ **Influencers**

❏ **Supporters**
❏ **Conceptualizers**
❏ **None of the above**

2. Which style makes the best leaders?
  ❏ **Drivers**
  ❏ **Influencers**
  ❏ **Supporters**
  ❏ **Conceptualizers**
  ❏ **All of the above**

3. Which style is the most creative?
  ❏ **Drivers**
  ❏ **Influencers**
  ❏ **Supporters**
  ❏ **Conceptualizers**
  ❏ **All of the above**

Now for the answers to the quiz:

1. There is **no best or worst** style! Each of us has a little of each of the four styles in us. There are successful people in all four styles. There are heads of state, CEOs, PhDs, medical doctors, sports legends, movie stars, authors, and people like you and me who come in all four styles.

2. Leaders come in **all four** of the styles! For example, General George Patton exhibited Driver tendencies. President John F. Kennedy exhibited Influencer

tendencies. President Abraham Lincoln and General Robert E. Lee exhibited Supporter tendencies. Albert Einstein exhibited Conceptualizer tendencies.

3. Creative people exist in **all four** styles! There are actors, inventors, and artists in all of the styles. For example, looking at the French Impressionist painters, Vincent Van Gogh displayed Driver tendencies, Claude Monet exhibited Influencer tendencies, Camille Pissarro showed Supporter tendencies, and Georges-Pierre Seurat demonstrated Conceptualizer tendencies.

People are resilient, adaptable, flexible, and changeable. As a situation changes, successful, mature adults can and do change. By being aware of the behavioral preferences we have, we can expand the menu of options available to us. We need not be limited to just those behaviors that lie inside our comfort zone.

> *"To improve is to change;*
> *to be perfect is to change often."*
> **Winston Churchill**

To use this book as it was designed, each person needs to determine which behavioral preference he or she exhibits most. Read the descriptions listed earlier in this chapter and determine which seems to describe you best. Remember, Drivers are exceedingly direct, task-oriented people who often check the time because they are busy. Influencers are talkative, socially outgoing people who tend to be the life of the party. Supporters are warm, relational, family-oriented people. They are calm, patient, and good listeners. Finally, Conceptualizers are analytical, detail oriented, and respectful of rules and regulations

Another way to determine your predominant behavioral style (and this is really a gross approximation) is to use this matrix.

If you tend to be: Fast Paced Mission Oriented **DRIVER**	**If you tend to be:** Fast Paced People Oriented **INFLUENCER**
If you tend to be: Reserve Paced Mission Oriented **CONCEPTUALIZER**	**If you tend to be:** Reserve Paced People Oriented **SUPPORTER**

As we mentioned earlier, each of us possesses all four of the behavioral tendencies found in Drivers, Influencers, Supporters, and Conceptualizers. Since behavior is situational, mature adults can adapt their behaviors. Still, each of us typically has one or two of these four traits that defines our behavioral comfort zone. During times of pressure or stress, we tend to revert to this comfort zone. For example, a Driver can adopt the characteristics of an Influencer if the job demands it. He can be outgoing, upbeat, and people oriented. However, if a crisis occurs, he is likely to abandon his Influencer traits and revert to the task-oriented, direct, fix-the-problem mode with which he is really more comfortable.

ACTION THIS DAY

1. Which behavioral style(s) do you tend to prefer most at work?

2. Which behavioral style(s) do you tend to prefer most at home? (They need not be the same as those at work.)

3. Is there a difference in the styles you prefer at work and at home? Why do you think there is a difference?

4. Can any of the strengths you have for your work focus be applied to your home focus, or vice versa?

Now that you understand how you tend to see the world based on your behavioral preferences, we are ready to look at the leadership methodology that Winston Churchill used. We will look at his methodology for each of the points of view: Driver, Influencer, Supporter, and Conceptualizer.

Each vignette focuses on a different aspect of Churchill's life. Each will be written in words that resemble closest the designated behavioral style. The questions at the end of each section are tailored to that reader's dominant or preferred style.

Here's the suggested approach: by reading the verbal descriptions of the four styles or using the matrix, determine which of the behavioral styles seems most like you.

Customizing *The Churchill Factors* for each reader:

All styles,
Read Part One (chapters 1-5),
Part Six (chapters 27-29), and Appendices

If you are a **Driver,**
also read Part Two (chapters 6-9)

If you are an **Influencer,**
also read Part Three (chapters 10-13)

If you are a **Supporter,**
also read Part Four (chapters 14-22)

If you are a **Conceptualizer,**
also read Part Five (chapters 23-26)

If you believe that you are equally strong in two of the styles, read the appropriate chapters for both. If you want the most complete discussion of the Churchill Factors, read all the chapters. The examples presented are different for each of the different styles. In Appendix I there are some additional applications for using this behavioral style technology.

Much of the information in this chapter was derived from the DiSC™ Dimensions of Behavior and the *Personal Profile System*® and *Focus Point*™ learning instruments developed and copyrighted by Inscape Publishing (formerly Carlson Learning Company). See Appendix III.

PART • TWO

In the Wilderness
(Especially for Drivers)

6

The Dropped Gauntlet

Drivers are bottom-line people. What is the formula for creating your finest hour? Use Winston Churchill's three proven principles for success: vision, courage, and determination. If you are a die-hard, "take no prisoners" Driver, that should be enough information for you to create your finest hour. If, however, you think you need a little more direction, then read on!

Challenges energize Drivers! The greater the challenge, the more opportunity there is to use your creative strengths. Creating your finest hour may be your greatest challenge.

"Where the rewards of valor are the greatest, there you will find also the best and bravest spirits among the people."
Xenophon

The challenge defines the task that has to be accomplished. We have to be clear concerning what exactly needs to be done. Once we can establish the boundaries of the challenge, we can press on to its achievement. This becomes our mission.

Winston Churchill's finest hour was the result of many challenges that he faced throughout his earlier life. His mettle was forged on the anvil of adversity. He had to overcome many overwhelming obstacles. Let's look at a struggle that must have seemed to him to last forever.

The flames of the Second World War grew out of the smoldering embers of the First. Churchill described the situation best: "...the void was open, and into the void after a pause strode a maniac of ferocious genius, the repository and expression of the most virulent hatred that has ever corroded the human breast—Corporal Hitler."

As the sinister undercurrents of militarism resurfaced in Germany, who would be willing to take a stand against the growing menace? The people were sickened by the last war, which had consumed a generation of Englishmen, Frenchmen, and Germans. Wouldn't it be far easier and less costly to appeal to the better judgment of Hitler than to confront him? One man didn't think so! That man was Winston Churchill.

A terrifying vision had formed in Churchill's mind. He foresaw grave consequences, not just to his nation but also to Europe and the entire world. He saw a world once again engulfed in a frightening war. Churchill, who had had a front-row seat at the carnage on the Western Front in World War I, felt compelled to avert another terrible world war. If he could only convince others in government of the perils, perhaps they could take a stand for peace and democracy. For Churchill, it all started with a vision.

It all starts with a vision for you, too. Before you set out on a trip, don't you need to know your destination? Knowing what you want to accomplish is the first element in creating your finest hour. This sounds simplistic, yet how many people really have a detailed idea of what they want to be, do, or have? The key word here is "detailed."

How detailed is enough? The more detailed, the better! Until you can establish specific, measurable results that are bounded by time, you will only be dealing with ambiguities. The old adage, "If you don't know where you are going, any road will take you there," still applies.

One approach is to think of a vision as a newspaper reporter would. The reporter would want to know the answers to the questions: who, what, when, where, why, and how. That would be detailed enough. That would hit the target!

Reporter's Approach:

**Who? What? When?
Where? Why? How?
Written with Headline**

This is not rocket science, but rather, a practical and executable approach. Let's look briefly at each of the elements of a vision.

Who: This could be you, your work group, your company, your industry, etc. In the foregoing Churchill example, the "who" would be the British Government.

What: This is a detailed description of the outcome or result that you want to attain. In our Churchill example, the "what" might be: the military forces of Britain must modernize and increase their weaponry and personnel as well as update their overall strategy and tactics.

Imbedded in the "what" is a means of tracking your progress. Are you getting closer to your objective or further away? There were several ways to track the progress. One could be the amount of the government's budget allotted to defense. Another could be the quantity of weapons or military personnel. Still another could be the time required for a military unit to deploy at full strength for a simulated crisis and achieve the designated objectives.

When: A "drop dead" time defines by when the vision must be achieved. In the Churchill example, the longer the British Government procrastinated in rearming, the more difficult it would be to catch up to Germany. In 1932, it might have taken the British two to three years. By 1940, Churchill was afraid it might be "too late"!

Where: This element adds specificity to the vision. In the Churchill example, "where" could encompass all military forces located in Great Britain as well as all forces located throughout the British Commonwealth.

Why: Next to the "what," the "why" is the most important element of a vision. The "why" tells the reasons the vision must be accomplished. The more compelling the reasons, the more likely the "whos" will do the "whats" by the "whens." In the Churchill example, there were many compelling reasons. Britain's survival as a free and independent nation was endangered by a militarily powerful and domineering Germany. The balance of power in Europe was unfavorably aligned against Britain. Britain was not able to protect her markets worldwide since her military forces were inferior to Germany's. Books have been written about the compelling reasons why Britain should have taken a stand against Germany in the mid-1930's.

How: Specific action steps break down the vision into smaller, more easily-accomplished actions. It's virtually impossible to swallow a vision in one gulp. There must be smaller, bite-sized portions that will nibble away at the task. (Drivers should not bite off more than they can chew!) Some of the thousands of action steps in our Churchill example could include: The British Government should increase military spending for more warships, airplanes, tanks, military personnel, etc. (Construction projects require long lead times.) Training for army, navy, and air forces must be increased in frequency, complexity, and responsiveness to projected threats. Get the picture?

Written: Since no one can remember all the details that define a well-constructed vision, it is imperative that all details be written down.

Now the reporter's approach to developing a vision is almost complete. A well-developed article has been written that includes all the pertinent information. The only thing that remains is a catchy headline or vision statement.

Headline: A vision statement should be short enough to be remembered, detailed enough to capture key facts, and compelling enough to make you take action. In our example, Churchill's vision statement might have been, "British Government to increase annual defense spending by 200% to counter Nazi threat!"

Creating Your Finest Hour
First Principle:

VISION

"If you can see it, you can paint it!"

Think of the vision as a painting. We could start splashing paint all over the canvas and just see what develops. But Drivers don't operate like that. We see the big picture first in our minds. We think about what needs to be done and by when. We are motivated to take action because of many compelling reasons. Before our paintbrush ever touches the canvas, we have the confidence that we can achieve our objective.

Drivers like to paint life boldly. They use strong, powerful colors. Their brushstrokes are direct and decisive. They work with speed. There is no picture too difficult for them to paint. They know they can do it!

ACTION THIS DAY

1. What are the greatest challenges in your life? (Career advancement, professional credentials and recognition, financial independence, etc.)

2. What are you committed to accomplishing in your life over the next five years that others have told you is impossible?

3. What qualities do you use to control the outcomes in your life that have brought you successes? (Being decisive, taking risks, taking charge, etc.)

4. Has there been any cost to you, your life, or those who mean most to you, in using these qualities? If so, what are some alternatives to getting results without sacrificing those important to you (including yourself)?

5. What words do you want on your tombstone?

Now that you have thought about who you are and what is important to you, let's take a few minutes and write out on a blank sheet of paper your vision for yourself. Select something you would like to accomplish within four months.

1. Who?

2. What? (Specific and measurable.)

3. When? (When you will achieve your outcome.)

4. Where?

5. Why? (List the compelling reasons why you must accomplish your vision. How about 10 reasons?)

6. How? (List some of the key action steps you will have to take to accomplish your vision.)

7. Headline: Write a vision statement (one you can memorize easily).

7

Stepping Out Boldly

The prologue to the classic "Star Trek" series began, "To boldly go where no man has gone before." This sounds like an ordinary day at work for most Drivers! Drivers are not tentative in words or deeds.

Once Drivers create a vision, they throw themselves into action. Their impulsiveness can either work for them or against them. If they have considered the possibilities and have enough of the details (the what, why, when, and how), then their leap off the starting block will give them some needed momentum. On the other hand, if they have not taken the time to consider the details, they may experience a false start.

What is it that distinguishes leaders from other people? Leaders have the courage to act. In fact, they are committed to taking action. This entails an element of risk. Drivers are no strangers to risk taking. They know that in order to attain any level of success, they have to take a risk.

> *"Success cannot be guaranteed.*
> *There are no safe battles."*
> **Winston Churchill**

To create a vision is relatively risk free. To put your vision into action takes courage. The world always stands ready to applaud a person for success and to condemn a person for failure. Those who have the courage to act despite their fears and the opinions of others open themselves to new opportunities. Isn't this the kind of effort that, over time, will create your finest hour?

> *"All men dream: but not equally. Those who dream by night in the dusty recesses of their minds wake in the day to find it was vanity; but the dreamers of the day are dangerous men, for they may act their dream with open eyes, to make it possible."*
> **T. E. Lawrence (of Arabia)**

During the 1930's, Winston Churchill had a vision for Britain's future. It entailed rearming and being able to stand up to any possible military provocation from Germany. Churchill was not a lightweight in British politics, nor was he a casual player as a member of the government. He had occupied a number of relatively senior positions of responsibility.

Churchill oversaw the Royal Navy for the three critical years before Britain's entrance into World War I and for more than the first year of the conflict. He later was in charge of the huge industrial engine that provided munitions, logistics, and supplies for the allied war efforts that overcame Germany. For a time after the war, Churchill was responsible for the army, the air service, and later the Colonial office. He also served as the fiscal administrator for the government and completed his fifth annual budget at the close of the 1920's. To say that Churchill was privy to the most important military, economic, foreign policy, and political decisions in Britain is an understatement.

The world of politics in which Churchill thrived resembles a river of frozen water more than it does solid ground. There were ample opportunities to slip and slide as well as fall through where the ice had become thin. Such a calamity happened to Churchill at a most critical time in history. A change in the government resulted in Churchill losing his cabinet position as Chancellor of the Exchequer. Furthermore, Churchill distanced himself from his own political party's move to grant independence to India.

Thus, for the third time in almost thirty years, he found himself without a position in the government. Suddenly the spigot of official information and intelligence was shut off. Churchill's opinion was neither solicited nor desired. He descended into a political wilderness.

Even though he was no longer directly responsible for the affairs of his nation, Churchill could not abandon his vision for Britain's welfare and ultimate survival. Rather than defer to the judgment of those in office, Churchill chose a route of high risk. He felt sure that a war was coming. He believed that it was his duty and chosen mission to warn his countrymen. He felt compelled to act.

Do you feel compelled to act on your vision? It takes courage to take that first step toward your vision. The first step is the most difficult, but isn't this what distinguishes the doers from the talkers? The talkers discuss what they intend to do. The doers simply do what has to be done. They take action and then don't fret about whether they should have acted in the first place.

> *"Never let the fear of*
> *striking out get in your way."*
> **George Herman (Babe) Ruth**

Short of war, sports offers us many appropriate analogies for living our lives. Most people have enough experience with sports in school that they can identify with the effort it takes to win a game as well as with the feelings one experiences after losing. It takes courage to get out of the bleachers and stand on the playing field. It takes courage to swing at the ball, knowing that even the best miss almost seventy percent of the time.

A person can approach a swing and a miss in two ways. He can revisit in his mind what happened and say, "Oh, I shouldn't have swung at that ball." Alternatively, he could say, "I missed that last one, but I won't miss the next one." One focuses on the past. The other is anticipating the outcome he desires in the future. Which approach will ultimately produce more hits?

Take that first step with courage and keep focused on your vision! Unlike the instant replay of every sports moment, you do not have time to revisit every decision you make. You need to keep pressing forward toward your goals.

Creating Your Finest Hour
Second Principle:

COURAGE

"Do it now, and don't look back!"

ACTION THIS DAY

1. Do you have a vision that no one else shares? Is your vision large and complex or smaller and easier to attain?

2. Do you feel compelled to act on your vision even though the risks of failure are great? Why?

3. What are the risks? What is their likelihood of actually occurring?

4. Do you revisit your decisions to act? Based on your past track record, does this instant replay assessment

result in more or fewer successful outcomes? Why do you think this is so?

5. What rituals or habits have you developed that help you take that first step toward your vision? What do you tell yourself (that is, what is your self-talk)?

8

Pressing On to the End

You created a vision. You have confidence in your own abilities to achieve it. You took that first step boldly and with courage. What do you need to do to make your vision a reality? You need to press on until you achieve it! Simple? Yes, but why do some people still have trouble achieving their dreams?

Drivers certainly believe they can tackle any challenge that comes their way. Somewhere between that first step and the last, there is a disconnect. Something sidetracks their efforts and derails their drive. Are we like a rock jutting out into the sea that is eventually worn away by the unceasing effects of winds and waves?

The loftier our vision, the longer it may take to attain it. The longer it takes, the more opportunities there are for obstacles to step into our path. Let's go to our example involving Winston Churchill.

Churchill thought a new European war was coming. Germany seemed to be the leading antagonist. At this critical time, Churchill found himself without a government post and was unable to tap into official sources of information. Rather than defer to those in power (who did not perceive any German threat), Churchill had the courage to warn his countrymen.

"The test of character is not 'hanging in' when you expect light at the end of the tunnel, but performance of duty and persistence of example when you know no light is coming."
Admiral James B. Stockdale

Courage means a person takes a stand for himself or others despite the possibility of a sacrifice of pleasure, happiness, or even existence. Churchill was a man of action and energy. He was not one to sit on the sidelines. He was always in the thick of the battle, whether inside the government or out. So what did he do? He took a stand and then never gave in.

Creating Your Finest Hour
Third Principle:

DETERMINATION

"Never give in!"

Churchill is best known for his bulldog determination. He simply would not give up. The British government and the British people thought he was crying wolf about the gathering storm clouds of war. Did he quit? No. He never gave in!

Several years later, Hitler attempted to bomb London into submission. Little did he know that Churchill was not just the Prime Minister, but also an empowering cheerleader. As the bombs dropped and the city suffered incredible damage, did Churchill and the people he represented quit? No, they never gave in!

"Let us therefore brace ourselves to our duties and so bear ourselves that, if the British Empire and its Commonwealth last for a thousand years, men will still say, 'This was their finest hour.'"
Winston Churchill

Determination means remaining in action, keeping the momentum going, and pressing on to the end. We can anticipate obstacles and distractions that will divert our attention from the outcomes we desire. We can expect to be thrown a variety of curve balls that will make us re-evaluate our swing.

Drivers can deal with change and risk. There will be no lack of either as we pursue our dreams. However, as long as we remain focused on the vision (remember all those compelling reasons "why"), then determination will enable us to cross the finish line.

A rowing coach knows that an oarsman will give up mentally before his body is physically exhausted. Determination means a person has the mental toughness to remain in action until his vision is achieved. How does a person develop mental toughness? There are four components involved.

The first component of mental toughness is preparation. We must be ready to play. Do we have the resources we need to embark on our vision? Have we adequately planned our quest? Are we organized enough to have the time to pursue our vision? During the development of our vision, we planned our action steps by establishing the "how."

The second component of mental toughness involves cultivating patience. As the effects of globalization increase, our demand for instant results increases. We want the shortcut. We want the bottom line. We want results immediately. We want it now!

"There is no instant pudding."
W. Edwards Deming

We must resist the temptation to accelerate our vision artificially. We must have the presence of mind, confidence, and character to work our visions at the appropriate pace. What is that pace? It's the one that gets the job done. It is constancy of purpose and consistency of action that will push us across the finish line.

In the sport of rowing (which is also called crew), the coxswain's real function is not to call out the pace or stroke, but rather to steer the boat and serve as the eyes for the oarsmen. The oarsmen are trained not to look at their competition during a race. Instead, they are to rely on the coxswain's verbal assessments, such as, "We're up half a length."

Furthermore, the oarsmen are told to row their own race and keep their eyes inside their own boat. While the competition may provide some added motivation to win, the real race is being fought inside each of the oarsmen's own minds. They are competing against themselves, based on their own standards of excellence. Of note, a sign used to hang in the locker room of UCLA's crew that said, "Conditioning is physical. Toughness is a state of mind. One without the other is a mockery."

Like the rowers, we need to row our own race and not be concerned about someone else's progress in their race. We keep our eyes inside our own boat. This is what patience is all about.

"You must never make a promise which you do not fulfill."
Winston Churchill

The third component of mental toughness involves promises. Accountability is the oil that allows determination to flow smoothly. We can make promises on two levels: with other people and with ourselves. We can share with family and friends our intention to remain in action until we achieve our vision. Sometimes this peer pressure may be sufficient for us to see the race through.

"The greatest victories are yet to be won,
the greatest deeds are yet to be done."
Theodore Roosevelt

The truly determined person makes a promise to himself or herself. However, keeping promises is more important than making them! This is the hallmark of champions. Champions keep their promises to themselves and others. Their personal integrity and self-discipline cause them to remain on course.

Preparation, patience, and promises require one additional component to enable a person to become mentally tough: practice. Vince Lombardi used to say, "Practice doesn't make perfect. Perfect practice makes perfect!" It is not enough to give our best effort. We can do the wrong things to the best of our abilities and not achieve our goals. Churchill once observed, "It is no use saying 'We are doing our best.' You have to succeed in doing what is necessary." We, therefore, must practice the appropriate activities correctly.

"Good ideas are not adopted automatically.
They must be driven into practice
with courageous patience."
Admiral Hyman G. Rickover

Practice also means having the willingness to stretch and grow. In much the same way that we pushed our behavioral comfort zones outward to strengthen our courage muscles, similarly we must stretch and grow in the determination arena.

We will use to the vision, courage, and determination methodology many times over a lifetime. We will learn from our mistakes. We will become more proficient at setting a vision, having the courage to take that first critical step, and following through with determination.

ACTION THIS DAY

1. What will you do every day to keep your vision alive?

2. What kinds of things make you impatient?

3. As you pursue your vision with vigor, what must you do to prevent your impatience from subverting your efforts?

4. List people with whom you feel safe to share your vision.

5. What promises will you make to these people?

6. What promises will you make to yourself?

7. As you make progress toward your vision, what things will you do to be mentally tough?

9

Climbing Out of the Valley

Let's look at a special application of this methodology. In life a person tends to find himself in one of three places: on level ground, on a mountaintop, or in a valley. When on level ground, a person is experiencing neither great success nor failure. This is the "business as usual" condition. A person is relatively comfortable when on level ground.

If the person has pursued some vision and has achieved some success, he may find himself on the mountaintop. The larger the success, the higher the mountain. Being on top of a mountain is a source of great exhilaration. There is a feeling of euphoria, confidence, and personal satisfaction. Oftentimes, one mountaintop experience is followed by another. Successes seem to occur in clusters. We must recognize, however, that mountaintop experiences are all ephemeral, fleeting events. There is always a higher mountain!

The biggest challenges we face occur when we are in the valley. The greater the challenge, the deeper the valley. A valley experience (also called a wilderness experience) is characterized by emotional lows such as anger, fear, failure, negativity, frustration, despair, rejection, sorrow, guilt, doubt, and depression. When we reach the deepest part of the valley, we may not even be able to see the sky. The canyon walls loom upward so steeply. We feel paralyzed to take any action. We've all had our valley experiences. Who can't say, "Been there. Done that. Got that tee shirt!"

"The ultimate measure of a man is not where he stands in moments of comfort and convenience, but where he stands at times of challenge and controversy."
Dr. Martin Luther King

Of the three domains—on level ground, on the mountaintop, or in the valley—where does a person grow the most? We grow when we choose to climb out of the valley. What do we need to do to get out of a valley experience? You guessed it: we need to use vision, courage, and determination!

We create a vision that shows us the way out of the valley. Then what? We need to have the courage and determination to climb out! On the climb out, don't be surprised if a number of setbacks or breakdowns occur. Imagine we're hiking up a steep path, and all of a sudden our shoes loose traction on the gravel-strewn path. We slide backward a short distance. Do we quit? Of course not! We continue to move upward with more discipline and dedication so that we don't slip again.

A breakdown offers us a test of our vision, courage, and determination. A breakdown should be considered an inconvenience, not a show stopper. Remember, the show must go on! Instead of letting a breakdown defeat us, we use it as an opportunity to recommit to our vision. Thus, when we have a setback, we don't quit, we recommit!

"Never give in! Never give in! Never, never, never, never—in nothing great or small, large or petty—never give in except to convictions of honor and good sense."
Winston S. Churchill

As we climb toward our vision with courage and determination, we may start to notice that we have changed since we fell into the valley. We look at our world and our lives differently. We are heading in a specific direction with intention. We have a compelling vision of what we want to be, do, or have. We have purpose, and we are committed to achieving our vision at all costs.

"No one who learns to know himself remains just what he was before."
Thomas Mann

Will it be easy to climb out of the valley? Probably not. Never underestimate the difficulty, but at the same time, do not let adversity defeat you. Those who climb out of the valley are incredibly stronger, emotionally and spiritually. We become transformed persons whose mettle was toughened by the hardships of the climb. Vision, courage, and determination will get us out!

ACTION THIS DAY

1. Have you had a recent valley experience? If so, what was it?

2. What was the hardest thing you had to deal with during that experience?

3. Were you able to climb out of the valley or are you still dealing with it?

4. What specifically did you do to climb out of the valley?

5. What did you learn from the climb out? What will you do differently next time?

6. How did your valley experience change you? What do you think or do differently now?

7. Is there someone you know who is presently in the valley? Can they benefit from what you have experienced?

8. How can increased sensitivity to other people benefit you professionally and personally?

9. What would be the impact on your success if you showed more tact, warmth, and understanding to others?

10. Because of your bottom-line focus, in what areas would you benefit from the help of others? (Who will weigh the choices you make? Who will keep the other people motivated about being on your team?)

PART ● THREE

A Grand Alliance
(Especially for Influencers)

Chapter 10: Allies for Possibility

Chapter 11: Being Vulnerable

Chapter 12: Pulling Out the Stops

Chapter 13: Conquering Procrastination

10

Allies for Possibility

Wouldn't you rather be visiting with a friend instead of reading a book? Perhaps you should find a friend who will read this section and relate it to you! Of course, you can also consider this a game, one in which you are competing against yourself. Do you have the discipline to win this game? If so, read on!

Influencers thrive in the presence of people. Face-to-face physical presence allows Influencers to see for themselves people and events, unfiltered by others' perceptions.

For Influencers, the best that life has to offer involves the unique relationships established among people. During Winston Churchill's long political career, he had extensive associations with many of the world's leaders and celebrities. These included George Bernard Shaw, several members of the Britain's royal family, Lawrence of Arabia, Dwight Eisenhower, and Harry Truman. One of Churchill's strongest friendships, however, was with U.S. President Franklin Delano Roosevelt (FDR).

When Churchill returned from the political wilderness to head the Royal Navy at the beginning of the Second World War, President Roosevelt asked Churchill to keep him informed of any developments. Churchill must have been overjoyed by such an overture. Little did FDR know that Churchill wanted him play a significant role in Britain's survival and future!

Churchill was a self-taught student of history. He possessed a keen understanding of the trends of history. He, more than any other world leader, foresaw and anticipated the calamity of war that Hitler exported across Europe. Because of his knowledge of the budget and the time it takes to construct ships, planes, and tanks, Churchill was keenly aware of Britain's precarious condition. The British had neither the resources, manpower, nor time to overcome the German menace.

Churchill also knew that President Roosevelt represented Britain's greatest hope. He knew that he would have to build rapport with the American president as well as develop a strong ongoing relationship with him. This became the nucleus of Churchill's vision concerning the survival of Britain.

"It is a mistake to look too far ahead.
Only one link in the chain of destiny
can be handled at a time."
Winston Churchill

Creating one's finest hour doesn't happen overnight. It happens over a lifetime of activity. Rather than just letting the future happen, a person prepares himself or herself to be ready when an opportunity occurs. We can use the methodology used by reporters to help in developing our vision. We can make a game out of this process. In fact, how well we play the game here will help us be more successful in the biggest game of all, the game of life.

Newspaper reporters are renowned for asking questions. There's power in questions! Many successful people have attributed their fortunes not to knowledge itself, but rather to their ability to ask the right questions and to act on what they learned.

Reporter's Approach:

Who? What? When?
Where? Why? How?
Written with Headline

Let's look at each of these elements as they would apply to the example involving Churchill and Franklin Roosevelt.

Who: Who are the players? In this case, Churchill and the British government are the players. Churchill, of course, is the star, and the government has a supporting role.

What: This involves what specific outcome or result is desired. In addition, there must be a way to track the progress of achieving one's vision. Churchill wanted to ensure Britain's survival when Britain and Germany had declared war on each other. He knew that Britain would need America's help. How can we find some yardstick to measure progress? One way might be the number of ships, guns, or ammunition America traded, loaned, or sold to Britain. Another way might be the number and warmth of the letters or telegrams Churchill received from FDR. Was FDR becoming friendlier, more supportive, etc.?

When: There needs to be a deadline to a vision, something to bound our efforts as well as create a sense of urgency. For Churchill the time limit was before it's "too late." This is a little general, but revealed the fears he had about his nation's future. Typically the "when" is some definite time in the future.

Where: This firms up our vision. Churchill couldn't expect FDR to visit him in Britain, but Churchill could meet the president in America and elsewhere in the world. Churchill knew that face-to-face meetings were always the best way to build a relationship with others. Telephone calls were the next-best method of communication. Letters and telegrams were the last resort for building rapport and cultivating relationships.

Why: Do you want your vision to succeed? If so, you will need many compelling reasons why you absolutely must achieve it. The more compelling reasons, the more likely you'll succeed! Churchill knew that Britain's survival depended on his winning FDR over. Imagine what survival means: saving family and friends, homes and businesses, way of life and heritage, culture and national treasures, and the like. You could easily find hundreds of reasons why Britain's survival was a must.

How: A series of action steps and when they must be achieved are needed. In simplest terms, Churchill wanted to build rapport with FDR. He needed to create an on-going dialogue with the American president. Most importantly, Churchill needed to visit face to face with FDR if he were to create a strong personal relationship with him.

Written: While Churchill probably didn't write out his vision, he certainly engraved it on his mind and his heart. If our visions are to be truly effective, we need to put our thoughts on paper. This makes it real. We need this working document to remind us as well as energize us when the going gets tough.

Headline: Let's pretend you're famous! You pick up the local newspaper and find an article about yourself on the first page. After you spend some time admiring the photo, you look at the headline. Did it say the right thing? You quickly read the article to see if they put in all the right information. Then you go back to the headline. A vision statement is your headline.

Your vision statement is a short description of what you want to achieve. For our Churchill example, it might read, "Churchill convinces American President in 1940 to help Britain defeat Hitler."

Think of your vision as a group of people who are painting together. You'll be working with your friends. You'll encourage each other as you cover the canvas with paint. Painting is fun! Think back to finger painting in kindergarten. You and your friends worked side by side. You used bright, exciting colors. Your movements were light and carefree. You entertained others in everything you did. Everything, however, started with a thought about what you wanted to paint on your canvas.

Creating Your Finest Hour
First Principle:

VISION

"If you can see it, you can paint it!"

ACTION THIS DAY

1. Which relationships mean the most to you? (Professional, social, or family) What do you do to keep these associations alive?

2. How important is social recognition to you when you develop a vision? With whom are you comfortable sharing your vision? Why?

3. How much do you rely on your gut feel when you make decisions involving your vision? Based on your past experiences, has your gut feel worked well for you?

4. By focusing more on people than on tasks, what kinds of things slip through the cracks when you set goals or plan for your future? Do you need to be more aware of time?

5. What fun things do you like to do? How can you make setting a vision fun? How can your co-workers, friends, and family help you in this area?

6. What do you want your friends to say about you after you pass away?

Now that you have thought about who you are and what's important to you, let's take a few minutes and write out on a blank sheet of paper your vision for yourself. Select something you would like to accomplish within four months.

1. Who?

2. What? (Specific and measurable.)

3. When? (When you will achieve your outcome.)

4. Where?

5. Why? (Compelling reasons why you absolutely must accomplish your vision. How about 10 reasons?)

6. How? (List some of the key action steps you will have to take to accomplish your vision.)

7. Headline: Write a vision statement (one that you can memorize easily).

11

Being Vulnerable

Influencers know that they place themselves at risk when they share information about themselves with others. It's important to come across to others in a positive light. Focusing on people can produce either social recognition and approval, or it can result in social rejection.

> *"He that loses wealth loses much;*
> *he who loses a friend loses more;*
> *but he who loses courage loses all."*
> **Miguel de Cervantes**

Winston Churchill understood that cultivating a personal relationship with Franklin Roosevelt wouldn't be easy. He knew that America was officially uncommitted to Britain in the early part of World War II.

In fact, while there were strong cries for America to remain isolationist as well as absent from European entanglements, Roosevelt was concerned whether Britain would fight or fold.

For Churchill, everything was riding on getting help from a neutral America. This entailed a measure of risk. He didn't know FDR well enough to know if Britain's requests would be favorably endorsed. The U.S. Ambassador to Great Britain, Joseph Kennedy (father of the future president), sent reports to FDR that essentially predicted Britain's defeat by Nazi Germany. Many of Roosevelt's other advisors gave less than comforting accounts about Churchill's personal habits. Despite these negative perceptions, Churchill chose to take that first step and communicate candidly, although cautiously, with the American president. That took courage on his part.

> *"To perceive a path and to point it out is one thing, but to blaze the trail and labor to construct the path is a harder task."*
> **Winston Churchill**

Churchill and Roosevelt had several fundamental differences of opinion as to how to fight the war and what the world would look like after the war. For example, Churchill was a strong advocate for the continuance of Britain's empire overseas while FDR believed otherwise. As America's involvement in the war became greater, Churchill's influence diminished. He realized that any hopes of Britain's regaining her earlier status as a world power rested with forming a strong postwar alliance with America. Thus, Churchill could probably foresee that while his initial vision of Britain's survival could be fulfilled, a longer-term vision of a partnership would require additional effort. It took courage on Churchill's part to risk public opinion at home while attempting to forge a postwar alliance with America.

Creating Your Finest Hour
Second Principle:
COURAGE
"Do it now, and don't look back!"

ACTION THIS DAY

1. Do you have a vision that others consider unrealistic? Is there any merit to their belief?

2. Are you more inclined to be spontaneous or measured in creating a vision? Why?

3. What is your greatest fear related to your vision?

4. How easy is it to transition from creating your vision to taking the action steps needed to achieve it? What can you do to overcome the inertia to take that first step?

5. How important is public approval in pursuing your vision? How can you use this recognition to motivate you to get started?

12

Pulling Out the Stops

The game has begun! You've overcome all resistance to inaction. The ball has been passed to you. You're now running down the field. The crowds are cheering for you! You can see the goal, but you also notice some obstacles cropping up in front of you. This could be a football game, or it could be you pursuing a compelling vision!

> *"Promises are the blowing of glittering bubbles; performances are the molding and hammering of iron."*
> **Winston Churchill**

In people-intensive visions such as Churchill's, the interpersonal dynamics may become increasingly complicated compared to the more mechanical, task-driven visions. Human interactions are simply more complex.

After Churchill decided to cultivate a personal relationship with Franklin Roosevelt, he knew that more than a handful of interactions would be needed. Even before he became Prime Minister on May 10, 1940, Churchill began to communicate regularly with FDR. In the five years between 1939 and Roosevelt's death in 1945, he sent the American president over 1,100 letters and telegrams. Roosevelt's replies numbered about two thirds as many. Churchill knew that written conversations were not enough.

Creating Your Finest Hour
Third Principle:
DETERMINATION
"Never give in!"

The evacuation of the British army from Dunkirk, the London Blitz, the threat of a German invasion, and the Battle of Britain in the skies kept Prime Minister Churchill occupied at home. He communicated in writing and by radio with FDR. Churchill's stirring speeches and bold actions certainly encouraged the American president.

In 1941, even though a war was raging in Europe, Churchill met with FDR in person twice. Once was during the drafting of the Atlantic Charter in late summer, and later, scarcely two weeks after the Japanese attacked the U. S. Pacific Fleet in Pearl Harbor. During that early winter visit, two remarkable events occurred that revealed the nature of Churchill's determination to cultivate FDR.

Churchill stayed at the White House for almost two weeks. On one occasion, FDR, who was crippled by polio (In 1934 Churchill noted, "His lower limbs refused their office."), wheeled himself into Churchill's room shortly after the Prime Minister had emerged from his bath. Churchill put on his best smile and reportedly said, "The Prime Minister of Great Britain has nothing to conceal from the President of the United States." Both men undoubtedly relished each other's wit, their similar backgrounds in leading their respective navies, and their past experiences with adversity. In addition, Keith Alldritt observed, "They were both connoisseurs of the English language."

> *"Do not let what you cannot do*
> *interfere with what you can do."*
> **John Wooden**

The second remarkable event occurred the day after Churchill addressed both Houses of Congress. He suffered a mild heart attack that should have put him in bed for six weeks. Even though Churchill did not know the full extent of his medical condition, he knew that he could not show that he was incapacitated for fear of losing American support. Thus, Churchill pressed on with his grueling schedule, even going to Ottawa to make a speech before returning to the White House for still more deliberations with FDR. Only Churchill's personal physician really knew how serious the Prime Minister's condition was.

Churchill and Roosevelt visited face to face on eight more occasions throughout the war. They headed major Allied strategy conferences in Casablanca, Teheran, Yalta, Quebec, and Washington, D.C.

Influencers share with Churchill the gift of communications. With their powerful persuasive skills, they are able to influence and inspire others. Looking inward, however, are you able to motivate yourself to remain in the game until you cross the finish line? Perhaps the cheers of the spectators will give you the drive needed to press on!

> *"Come then, let us go forward*
> *together with our united strength."*
> **Winston Churchill**

ACTION THIS DAY

1. What do you say to motivate yourself? Can the words you use to encourage others also inspire you?

2. What will you do every day to keep your vision alive? How will you reward yourself for completing key action steps?

3. What kinds of things would sidetrack your progress toward your vision? (For example, details, deadlines, or inability to follow through.) What can you do to prevent this?

4. How can you press on to the finish line, including paying attention to the details, and enjoy doing it?

5. How can you involve others in your vision to encourage you? What promises will you make to these people?

13

Conquering Procrastination

Maintaining our momentum is a remedy for self-doubt. Moving forward is also a key solution to the brother of self-doubt, procrastination. We have all experienced procrastination. How can we slay this dragon?

Procrastination is frequently the result of being overwhelmed by complex or unpleasant actions we must take. We may want to avoid making critical decisions or taking necessary actions. Shouldn't we uncover the real identity of procrastination?

"Procrastination is the thief of time."
Edward Young

Procrastination is a thief! It steals from you the most precious, nonrenewable resource there is: time! It diverts your attention from the important to the unimportant. The old saying, "Time is money," would be more accurate if we said, "Time is life!" All the wealth in the world cannot buy a dying man more time. As we get older, time seems to run faster and faster for us.

When, as a child,
I laughed and wept,
Time crept.

When, as a youth,
I dreamed and talked,
Time walked.

When I became a
full-grown man,
Time ran.

And later,
as I older grew,
Time flew.

Soon I shall find,
while traveling on,
Time gone.

Will Christ have saved
my soul by then?
Amen.

Inscription on a clock in Chester Cathedral, England

The consequences of procrastination ultimately impact your life. Procrastination is a thief that robs you of your life!

The seeds needed to defeat procrastination were already planted in the development of our vision. Remember the compelling "whys"? These gave us the motivating fuel to continue our great race. Remember the "hows"? These were the action steps that broke down the vision into manageable pieces that could be accomplished more easily.

Procrastination causes great emotional turmoil. When we postpone a task, we are also are postponing the relaxation that comes when the job is done. We remain anxious and tense until the task gets completed. Guilt dogs our heels. On the other hand, when we don't procrastinate, and we do a job right away, we give ourselves the satisfaction, relief, and freedom from anxiety that come as an added bonus of accomplishing a task.

If you want to conquer procrastination, then get mad at it! Don't let it rob you of your life! What was our courage principle? "Do it now and don't look back!" This is an antidote for the poisoning effects of procrastination. Keep moving toward your vision with courage.

"Time is neutral; but it can be made the ally of those who seize it and use it to the full."
Winston Churchill

ACTION THIS DAY

1. What kinds of things do you tend to put off?

2. Think about one thing (something that you could be or do) that if you became or did, would significantly change the course of your life. (For example, you want to become an author.) Now fill in that answer at the end of the sentence below. (For example, procrastination is a thief that robs the best of authors.)

PROCRASTINATION is a thief that robs the best of _____

3. How does the answer to question two make you feel?

4. What are the consequences of procrastinating in this area?

5. What do you intend to do to take back control of your time so you can do what is crucial to you?

6. If you conquer procrastination in this one important area, what will be the payoff for you? List ten reasons why you must take back control.

7. When will you start?

PART • FOUR

The Landscape of Leadership
(Especially for Supporters)

14

It All Starts with a ...

Supporters are comfortable in a safe environment in which they do what they have done before. They prefer the status quo to the uncertainties of change, because change entails risks and the possible loss of stability. When a chain of new events cascades into Supporters, they may seek to slow down the pace until they can regain that feeling of safety and stability.

We do have the ability to influence our future in a way that is not threatening to our basic assumptions about life. We can make change be an ally and not something to be avoided. Furthermore, we can condition ourselves to adjust our views and feelings about new possibilities.

Let's use the painting analogy to illustrate ways we can adapt to change. Painting a landscape on a canvas is similar to rediscovering the masterpiece that exists in all of us.

"We are always changing, like nature we change a great deal, although we change always very slowly. We always change, and consequently we are always reaching a higher level after each change, but yet with the harmony of our life unbroken and unimpaired."
Winston Churchill

We spoke earlier about putting the past in the past. This entailed shedding some of the emotional baggage we carry with us. Forgiveness was one of the ways to prevent us from wasting emotional energy that kept us from moving forward. We can give ourselves permission to start again wherever we are. We can begin with a clean, unpainted canvas.

A blank canvas stares back at you! It's intimidating, but this is a normal reaction. Many an artist hesitates when standing before a blank white canvas. What if he makes a mistake? Maybe he should not start until he knows he can paint his canvas perfectly. Have you ever been overwhelmed like this, when starting something new?

One way an artist may deal with an intimidating white canvas is to prime it with some soft, subdued colors. That will remove some of the glare, but more importantly, it will get us out of the mindset of not being afraid to start. So let's prime our canvas before we begin our painting.

"Difficulties mastered are opportunities won."
Winston Churchill

It takes personal leadership to create your finest hour. No one but you can do this. All the positive or negative encouragement in the world cannot make you take any action that you choose not to do. Personal leadership is an inner motivation that propels you forward to take some action. Let's take a minute and briefly discuss leadership.

If you read newspaper or magazine interviews with everyone from international celebrities to the man on the street, you come away with one basic conclusion about leadership: leadership is all things to all people. One person's opinion about leadership may be radically different from the views held by another. Even among a group of leaders, there may be little agreement as to what constitutes the best way to lead. In this sense, leadership is more an art than a science.

I want to draw an important distinction between leadership and personal leadership. Personal leadership involves only yourself. Before you can hope to influence someone else, you must first deal with the person you see in the mirror. Leadership on this micro (i.e., individual) level involves the same basic elements that are needed on the macro (i.e., group) level. The actions you will take individually will be similar to the kind taken when involving many people. To avoid confusion, I will refer to leadership on the micro level as "personal leadership" and leadership on the macro level simply as "leadership."

As stated earlier, there are libraries of books on how to develop the leader in you. With careful study and discipline, you can train yourself to develop the proper reflexes and responses. Trial and error will help you hone your skills. But maybe you're the kind of person who says, "I don't have two months to read and study a book. What can I do right now?"

That's a good question! Personal leadership, as well as leadership in the larger sense, takes place on the playing field of life. Personal leaders do not sit safely in the stands watching the game. Instead, they place themselves at risk by getting down on the field. People can and will judge you when you are down on the field. Playing in the game of life, however, means moving the ball down the field. Sometimes you will be able to score a point and sometimes you won't. Either way, personal leadership involves some action on your part.

> *"Change your thoughts and*
> *you change your world."*
> **Norman Vincent Peale**

You picked up this book because you want to be a better player. Okay, so where do we start? Personal leadership starts with a thought. The thought is essentially, "What do I want to do?" Nothing earth-shaking there! Think back to our painting analogy. The artist finds a blank canvas staring back at him. Assuming the artist doesn't just want to copy what he sees before him, there are several additional questions the artist may ask. "How do I feel about the scene? What do I want to capture on the canvas? How much detail shall I show? Why am I painting this scene anyway?"

Sometimes we have to back into what we want to paint on our canvas. Perhaps we don't like the scene we see. Maybe we want to employ a little artistic license and add a tree, or enlarge a stream, or move a mountain. The artist has the ability to change a scene if the one before him doesn't suit him. How about in real life? Are you limiting yourself in any way?

"Painting is a friend who makes no undue demands, excites to no exhausting pursuits, keeps faithful pace even with feeble steps, and holds her canvas as a screen between us and the envious eyes of time or the surly advance of decrepitude."

Winston Churchill

Now let's have Winston Churchill enter the stage. In 1915, following his traumatic removal from office as the head of the Royal Navy, he looked for a way to divert his mind from the politics, confusion, and emotions of a stalemated world war. Churchill had become a political scapegoat for the military efforts in Turkey (the Dardanelles and Gallipoli Campaigns in World War I). Noted naval historian Arthur Marder once told this writer that Churchill's plan was "the most brilliant strategic initiative of the entire war." (If Admiral Farragut had been at the Dardanelles instead of the British admiral, perhaps the course of world history would have been different!) The politicians had taken away more than Churchill's position in the government. They had robbed him of his confidence, his identity, and his self-esteem. Churchill now had time on his hands, and he turned to painting to salve his grief.

"We have before us a great opportunity, a golden opportunity, glittering bright but short lived. Our chance is now at hand. The chance is there; the cause is there, the man is there."
Winston Churchill

During his first attempt at oil painting, Churchill found himself staring at a blank white canvas. The bold, decisive leader was overwhelmed with what to do first. He was cautious, because he feared he might make a mistake. He tentatively put a small dab of blue paint on the canvas and then considered the result. As he pondered his next "bold" move, an artist friend happened to visit him. She grabbed a large brush, jabbed it into some paint, and slashed it across the canvas with vigorous strokes. Churchill was amazed that the canvas did not strike back! That broke the spell. Churchill then began to paint again, this time not paralyzed by his fears.

He had a vision of himself creating landscapes of beauty. Painting began as a pastime; it became a blessed relief from the strains of a demanding life. Churchill would complete over six hundred paintings between this timid start and his retirement from political life some forty years later. (Because of the demands on him as

Prime Minister, he painted only once during the Second World War, in Marrakech after the Casablanca Conference with Roosevelt.) For Churchill, painting became, to use his words, "bottled sunshine." It brought the brilliant light of creativity and activity to an overworked mind darkened by heavy responsibilities.

"I cannot pretend to feel impartial about colors. I rejoice with the brilliant ones and am genuinely sorry for the poor browns. When I get to heaven, I mean to spend a considerable portion of my first million years in painting and so get to the bottom of the subject. But then I shall require a still gayer palette than I get here below. I expect orange and vermilion will be the darkest and dullest colors and beyond them there will be a whole range of wonderful new colors which will delight the celestial eye."
Winston Churchill

Churchill had a colorful vision of his future. Do you still have a vision of yourself? It all starts with a vision.

15

Reporting On Your Future

What is a vision anyway? A vision is a thought. It is a picture of something you want to be, do, or have. It is an expectation you want to fulfill. Don't get caught up in all the jargon and semantic hair-splitting! Vision, dream, expectation, goal, objective, result, outcome, and the like, all refer to the same basic idea. So before you can get emotionally excited enough to actually do something, you must first have a vision or thought of what you want to do.

"Vision is the art of seeing things invisible."
Jonathan Swift

Failure to specify what you want to be, do, or have is just like a ship steaming across the ocean without a rudder. The ship is at the mercy of the winds and currents and maybe even to imbalances in the engines. Having a vision sets a specific course to follow.

Developing your vision should be more than just a fun activity. It should energize you. If it doesn't, then perhaps what you imagine yourself doing is not something you are really committed to achieving. Unless you are willing to take all the necessary steps to achieve your vision, the process may become tedious and demoralizing instead of thrilling and rewarding.

There are many ways to create your vision. I will suggest one to get you started. Pretend you have your own newspaper. You are the publisher, editor, reporter, advertiser, and reader. Any article in your newspaper must be newsworthy. If a story is dull and boring, will you want to read it? Of course not! Similarly, your vision must be newsworthy.

When you read a newspaper article, you expect to find answers to questions involving who, what, when, where, why, and how. These are the same questions you must answer about your vision.

Reporter's Approach:

Who? What? When?
Where? Why? How?
Written with Headline

Let's look briefly at each one and use as an example Churchill's painting hobby.

Who: This can be you, your spouse, your family, your work group, your company, your industry, etc. Typically this would be you. In our example, it was Churchill.

What: This refers to the specific details of your vision. What do you want to be, do, or have? The more detailed you make your vision, the better. Churchill's vision was to find some relief from the demands of his chosen profession and the outside world. He needed something compelling enough to capture his attention and divert it from the emotional intensity of being a government servant.

When crafting your "what," think how you can measure your success. Are the actions you will be taking getting you closer to your vision? There needs to be some yardstick to help you track your progress. In Churchill's case, he could have used his blood pressure, number of headaches per day, or number of days when he felt depressed as possible barometers of not achieving his vision. It is unlikely he actually used these measures. He probably noticed that he felt better, was more relaxed, and that painting steadied and refreshed him.

If your vision isn't measurable, it will be more difficult to track your progress. You can be creative here and use yardsticks that are as unconventional as necessary: furlongs per fortnight, number of hugs per day, pounds per month. Your "what" then becomes a specific, measurable result.

When: A vision should be bounded by a specific time interval. The "by when" is what transforms intentions into a promise or commitment. Open-ended visions simply do not have the power and strength of a vision that must be accomplished by a specific time. Giving your dream a definite deadline prevents you from slacking off when the inspiration and excitement of your vision start to cool. Churchill needed some relief right away. Typically your vision will be long term, for example, from three months to a year. You need enough time to allow things to work. If the "by when" is too short (only a few weeks), you may not have enough time to see results, and then, frustration and disappointment may set in.

Where: In the world of vision, the "where" is another detail that gives solidity to the vision. Newspaper articles specify a dateline, that is, where the action occurred. So should you. Churchill painted wherever his work took him. He painted all over the world, starting in 1915 and continuing until 1960 (when he was eighty-five).

Why: Do you want to give some thrust to your vision? When you add some compelling reasons why you absolutely *must* accomplish it, it is equivalent to strapping a high-octane rocket on your back! The "whys" define the context or basis of your vision. They specify the reasons you are willing to sacrifice your time, your talents, and your treasure to accomplish your vision.

Purpose without passion resembles a crew racing shell without oars. Not only will you go nowhere fast, you'll never even leave the starting line! A list of ten, twenty, or even fifty powerful reasons why you absolutely *must* achieve your vision will provide enough compelling fuel to rocket you to your desired outcome!

"If the why is big enough, the how is no problem."
Nietzsche

Using our example involving Churchill, he needed an outlet to give him some relief from his demanding lifestyle. The biggest reason was to maintain his sanity. He wanted something that would let him recharge his batteries without having to rely on the outside world.

How: Don't play Superman! Most visions are too large to accomplish in a single bound. You will need a series of smaller action steps to reach your desired outcome. You will need near-term and long-term action steps to accomplish your vision. The "how" becomes your action plan that specifies the discrete steps you will take as you climb to the mountaintop of your vision.

Churchill's action steps involved some study on his own as well as coaching from others. He practiced his painting and amused himself with still life paintings, *en plein air* landscapes (i.e., painted outdoors, not in a studio), and paintings made by copying photographs. He toured museums with artist friends and studied the paintings of the great masters. He practiced painting while being coached by other artists.

Written: As you develop your vision, think of yourself as a reporter working on a Pulitzer Prize-winning story. In your story you will include the who, what, when, where, why, and how. Does the reporter keep the story solely in his head? No, he writes it down. You too must get your vision down on paper. The difference between a vision and a daydream is that a vision is real enough to touch. You can show yourself and others your vision when it is written down. Your written vision will probably be several sentences, paragraphs, or pages long—whatever it takes to describe it accurately.

Headline: What do you need to attract readership to your story? You need a catchy headline. This becomes your vision statement. Your vision statement should be short enough for you to memorize. After all, it is already engraved on your mind and heart. For Churchill, perhaps it was, "Painting comes to the rescue of an overworked statesman. Ten paintings expected this year." Your vision statement will need to be a little more detailed. Incorporating the who, what, when, and whys in it will tell you and others exactly where you are headed.

16

Eating What You Can Chew

All too often, vision setters bite off more than they can chew. Setting too lofty or difficult a vision can be more harmful than setting none at all. Are you making it easy for yourself to succeed, or are you sabotaging your chances of success? Don't forget that old football adage, "The first rule of winning is, don't beat yourself!" Our vision should challenge us, not discourage us!

> *"A man can succeed at almost anything*
> *for which he has unlimited enthusiasm."*
> **Charles Schwab**

Your vision should *gently* stretch you out of your comfort zone. Just as an athlete would never think of working out without first warming up, you must carefully condition yourself in setting your vision. This means you will have to be a *little* more creative, a *little* more energetic, and a *little* more persevering. A vision causes us to grow. We grow in ability, in experience, and most importantly, in confidence.

The process of creating an empowering vision is a means to help you succeed, not an opportunity to make you fail. As your achievement muscles strengthen, you will be able to refine or set even more challenging visions for yourself. Remember, all of us must walk before we learn to run.

"Don't be afraid of going slowly, be afraid of standing still."
Chinese Proverb

It is the *process* of pursuing your vision that is more important than its actual achievement. In other words, it is the journey, not the destination, that transforms our lives. Once you achieve your vision, set a new one. Keep moving the ball down the field! Successful people know that repeating the process of setting and achieving visions will, over time, represent a massive change when all is summed up.

Do you visualize seeing yourself achieve your vision? This is a powerful technique to precondition your mind for success. Try to imagine seeing yourself after accomplishing your vision. There's a smile on your face. Your voice is confident and outgoing. As the sunlight streams through your office window, the scent of freshly-cut gardenias in a delicate crystal vase reminds you of the sweet fragrance of success. You can almost hear the coins jingling in your pockets! Engage as many of your senses as possible as you visualize your way to the top.

Do you want to achieve more? Then visualize more! Whatever you consistently focus on, you will achieve! Visualize achieving your vision when waking up, before going to sleep, and several times throughout the day. Visualizing is not idle daydreaming, but rather intentionally rehearsing the future you want to create!

"Extraordinary people visualize not what is possible, but rather what is impossible. And by visualizing the impossible, they begin to see it as possible."
Cheri Carter-Scott

Our vision thus becomes the outcome we hope to fulfill. Instead of waiting hopefully for something to occur, we have reversed the process and defined specific and measurable results we want to achieve. Our vision defines our hope and becomes the first step in creating our finest hour.

17

Opening the Filters

Having a vision means seeing our hope in our mind's eye. To get there, we must take the long view. It is not something we can achieve in two hours. (Visions usually entail a long-term commitment, probably on the order of weeks, months, or years.)

Imagine a ship at sea. It leaves port and journeys over the ocean toward a destination that is miles away. The captain on the bridge of the ship can only see so many miles to the horizon. His destination (his vision) is over the horizon. As the ship travels, the captain makes adjustments to his course based on the strength of winds, seas, and currents, thus altering his originally planned track. Even though the destination is not directly seen, if the captain applies these corrections, the ship will eventually arrive at its destination.

We do essentially the same thing with our vision. We take a long view since it will take a period of time to achieve our vision. To use one of President Reagan's expressions, "We must stay the course."

"Long-term victory happens one day at a time."
Beth Moore

Wouldn't it be useful for the captain to see what is going on beyond his visual horizon? To do this means developing over-the-horizon sight. By gaining a higher perspective, he can see farther. The same applies to our vision process. Just as our vision is limited when we are right on the surface of the ocean, our vision is also bounded by the filters that shield our eyes and minds from new information.

These filters are given a fancy name: paradigms (pronounced *pair-ah-dimes*). In essence, these filters allow you to see things with which you are familiar or comfortable. Actions that fall outside these parameters may be rejected. Let me give you an example. My idea of a hamburger is a round piece of meat on a bun. One of my sons, however, who flipped burgers for Wendy's, became comfortable with their square burgers. In fact, on busy nights when he ran out of meat, he was really upset at having to obtain some "circle meat." My son's hamburger paradigm was a square burger. (At Wendy's, they don't cut corners!)

Developing over-the-horizon sight means opening more widely the filters of our eyes and minds to new ideas and possibilities. To do this we may have to change our perspective, that is, look at things from a different viewpoint. Looking at things from a different viewpoint may make things clearer for us. This is especially important if we become lost or confused as we travel toward our vision.

One of the most important paradigm shifts each of us needs to make involves the way we see ourselves. All of us have an internal estimate of how much we think we can accomplish in our lifetime. If we work diligently for thirty or forty years or so, we hope to retire and live comfortably. We can imagine ourselves moving up the ladder of success during our working years. It's all very orderly and predictable in our minds.

"You can never cross the same river twice."
Colin Fletcher

The real world, however, is not predictable. Some businesses merge, some are bought out, and some fail. Health may not remain manageable. Severe weather, workplace mishaps, or tragic accidents can pull the rug out from under us. Violence, calamity, and poverty, like rain, fall on the just and the unjust. While we cannot control most of the random things that happen to us, we can control who we are and how we react to events.

Who we are and what we can be is directly related to our self-esteem. The U.S. Army has marketed itself with the expression, "Be all you can be." Most people understand that each of us uses only a fraction of his or her potential. But who we are is limiting in itself. Most of us simply do not know what we are truly capable of being or doing. If we consider the possibility that we can be more than we ever imagined we could be, then we can push our performance envelope outward. Do you see the difference between this belief and the one used by the U.S. Army? Don't most of us tend to underestimate ourselves? If we are to create our finest hour, we need to expand our vision of ourselves.

Creating Your Finest Hour
First Principle:
VISION
"If you can see it, you can paint it!"

In art, as in life, there are many ways to paint the same scene. Supporters prefer a softer, gentler approach to their paintings. They like to use warm, friendly, harmonious colors. They are sensitive to the world around them, and it shows in their paintings. Their pace is calm, and they proceed step by step until they finish.

> *"If you really know what you want out of life,*
> *it's amazing how opportunities will come*
> *to enable you to carry them out."*
> **John M. Goddard**

Regardless of the approach we use to paint our life's masterpiece, we must first picture in our mind what outcome we want. If we can see that picture in our minds, we can paint it on our canvas. Thus, our compelling vision, which began as a thought in our minds, will become the fuel that will propel us toward our finest hour!

18

Creating Your Vision

Your vision can be as large or as small as you need. Some people have a vision for their lives. Others may have a vision of what they hope to accomplish over the next year. Still others may just have a vision of what they desire to achieve during the next three months.

> *"When I paint, I have the feeling that my eyes are reborn. I now see things that I never saw before."*
> **Dwight D. Eisenhower**

The good news is that the methodology is basically the same, whether the span of time is ten years or ten weeks. Most of us would benefit, however, from expanding our horizons. We tend to underestimate our potential, and thus, we sell ourselves short.

Perhaps we can push the envelope outward by thinking about our vision from a larger point of view. The following questions are designed to help you see yourself in terms of a bigger picture. These are important questions because when a person can gain a new insight about himself or herself, it is possible that his or her life can be changed in a powerful way. Don't forget the "butterfly effect."

ACTION THIS DAY

1. What do you stand for? (For example, integrity, freedom, achievement, happiness, etc.)

2. What are you committed to? (For example, making a difference, personal growth, family, etc.)

3. If you could be any person in the past, who would you be? What qualities of this person do you admire most?

4. If you could be anything you wanted and knew you couldn't fail, what would you be? Why?

5. What legacy would you like to leave on this planet?

6. Which of your achievements or future achievements would you like to be acknowledged by other people?

7. How would you like your obituary to read?

Now that you have thought about who you are and what is important to you, let's take a few minutes and write out on a blank sheet of paper a vision for yourself. Select something you would like to accomplish within the next four months.

1. Who?

2. What? (Specific and measurable.)

3. When? (When you will achieve your outcome.)

4. Where?

5. Why? (Compelling reasons why you absolutely must accomplish your vision. How about 10 reasons?)

6. How? (List some of the key action steps you will have to take to accomplish your vision.)

7. Vision Statement. (Now you have a detailed, written vision. What headline will you give it?)

19

Taking That First Step

How do we transform our vision into reality? This brings up the second key principle, courage. Remember, vision begins in our minds. Courage, however, begins in our hearts. When someone mentions courage, we think of bravery, boldness, gallantry, valor, and fearlessness. Most of these words are associated with physical courage, such as we might find on the battlefield. Courage, however, has many facets.

Consider this example. Imagine a piece of sturdy wood, three feet wide and fifty feet long, placed across cinder blocks two feet high. It's a small bridge just two feet off the ground. If you were standing on one end, and a $1,000 bill were taped in the middle, would you be able to walk across the bridge and pick up the $1,000 bill? Most of us would answer that we would. The three-foot-wide bridge seems wide enough.

Now take the same bridge—still three feet wide—and have it rest across the two sides of the Grand Canyon. Now the bridge is suspended approximately *one mile* off the ground. Would you retrieve the $1,000 bill taped to the middle? Probably not! The bridge is the same size, but its height above the ground is different. The risks are much greater in the second case. Can you imagine any reason why you might overcome the risk to walk to the center of the bridge?

Consider this scenario. We have the same physical arrangement as before. The wooden bridge is three feet wide and suspended over the Grand Canyon. You are at one end. In the middle, your 3-year-old child is trying to pick up the taped $1,000 bill. You'd venture out on the bridge to rescue your child, wouldn't you?

"Necessity does the work of courage."
George Eliot (Mary Ann Evans)

People can do extraordinary things when the situation so demands. A parent will take almost any risk to save his or her child. What does it take to step outside our personal comfort zone and risk everything? It takes courage.

Let's get back to harnessing hope and creating our finest hour. You are the only one who can decide to escape from your past into your future. The choice is up to you, and it takes courage.

Courage is like a muscle. We develop it by using it. A useful analogy is that of the weight lifter. How do weight lifters build strength? They do it by progressively increasing the amount of weight they lift. The same thing applies to courage. The more we use it, the stronger we will become.

Soldiers in wartime report that physical courage is contagious. Putting raw recruits with experienced soldiers conditions the recruits to be more courageous. If a select few of the natural leaders are courageous, the whole unit will follow suit and charge a hill despite a punishing frenzy of hot lead and cold steel by the enemy. That's physical courage.

"If there is something that you think you can do, even dream that you can—begin it! Boldness has mystery and power and magic in it."
Goethe

Moral courage, or the courage to follow one's convictions, is a battle fought inside one's head and heart. Here the strength of a person's values is weighed against the possibility of failure, embarrassment, ridicule, humiliation, rejection, and the like. If your values, such as family, honesty, integrity, health, or making a difference, are compelling enough, there will be no question in your mind what course to follow.

"I have no fear of the future. Let us go forward into its mysteries, let us tear aside the veils which hide it from our eyes, and let us move onward with confidence and courage."
Winston Churchill

Churchill's paintings were initially just private efforts. Later he worked with other painters who critiqued his works. Still later he exhibited his works under a pseudonym. Eventually he gave paintings to presidents and royalty. Today, his paintings command handsome sums, and many adorn the valued collections of respected museums. Clearly Churchill gained both confidence and ability as an artist. But before he ever put a brush to canvas, he had to have the courage to take that first step.

20

... Is the Thing!

Courage is the principal catalyst in all human activity. While mankind has been abundantly blessed by people with vision, the movers and shakers of the world were the ones who transformed their visions into reality. That took courage.

"It is not because things are difficult that we do not dare; it is because we do not dare that they are difficult."
Lucius Annaeus Seneca

One of the most common reasons for not taking an action is fear. Some examples are fear of the unknown, fear of failure, fear of embarrassment, or even fear of success. One commonly-held belief is that a courageous person has no fear. While some people (for example, Navy fighter pilots or SEALs) may have an unusually high fear threshold, fear is a normal, human self-defense mechanism. Courageous people act in the presence of fear. They recognize and acknowledge their fears but have learned (that is, conditioned themselves) to respond even in the presence of fear.

Are there ways to develop courage? When I was in the Navy, one of my commanding officers used the expression, "Do it now!" I can't tell you how many times I heard, "Do it now!" (I even started to tell my kids to "do it now.") Courage means "do it now, and don't look back!" Take that first step, and don't revisit your decision to act.

Creating Your Finest Hour
Second Principle:
COURAGE
"Do it now, and don't look back!"

Is this risky business? Yes, but life is a risk. Courage means a person is committed to taking action. Thinking about a vision means absolutely nothing unless that first step is taken. Sir John Barrie, author of *Peter Pan*, said it best, "Courage is the thing! All goes if courage goes!"

Organizations that develop and cultivate leaders know that effective leaders have the courage to act. Proven leaders have singled out the courage to act as the most important trait a leader can possess (ahead of vision, integrity, communications skills, adaptability, etc.). Leadership, both on a personal level and on a group level, involves taking some action. Courage enables a leader to take that first step.

"Courage is rightly esteemed the first of human qualities because it is the quality which guarantees all others."
Winston Churchill

Taking that first step means stepping outside our personal comfort zone. When we are comfortable, we are not inclined to change our circumstances. Harnessing hope and creating our finest hour mean that in order to give life to our vision, we must be willing to grow.

Why are people reluctant to step out of their personal comfort zone? We are afraid of making a mistake. The idea of zero defects has created a phobia that inhibits creativity, innovation, and leadership. There are some legitimate zero defect occupations. Nuclear safety is one. Brain surgery is another. Zero defects mean perfection. Most of life, however, does not demand perfection.

Striving for perfection will cause a vision seeker to wait until everything is just right. Now hear this: perfection will paralyze your performance. Did you get that? Wanting to be perfect will paralyze you. It will keep you from taking action.

Finding a happy balance between perfection and risk-taking brings us to the idea of excellence. Excellence means that there are high standards of performance, but people are encouraged to discover new (and hopefully better) ways of doing things. Creativity and innovation can make business processes more user-friendly, less redundant, and more timely.

Excellence further acknowledges that we may make mistakes. But isn't that how we learn? Isn't that how we develop good judgment? We must give ourselves permission to make mistakes and to learn from them.

Think for a moment about an artist painting his masterpiece. Suppose he took that first step, and the result was not exactly what he wanted. Then what? The artist can stop and consider his options. He can fix what he did. He can create something new out of his mistake. Perhaps his mistake was nothing more than a "happy accident." Of course, he can always scrape off the paint and start over again. These same options are also open to us as we create our finest hour.

> *"Vision without action is an illusion.*
> *Action without vision is confusion."*
> **Willie Jolley**

How did John Grisham produce all those bestsellers? He got past the first page and kept on writing. He literally put one word in front of another and repeated the process. It all began, however, with that first word. Remember, the water does not start to flow until you turn on the faucet!

ACTION THIS DAY

1. What concerns do you have as you pursue your vision? Whom do you trust for encouragement and moral support?

2. What can you do to condition yourself to change? What can you do to have a calming influence on others? How can you calm yourself?

3. Supporters can find all their energy reserves dedicated to the needs of others. What can you do to have sufficient time and energy to serve your personal needs?

4. Supporters are extremely effective listeners. How can you use these skills to learn from others? In particular, what clues can you learn from other people about how to overcome your fears?

5. Do you feel more comfortable making a decision by yourself or as part of a team? Why? Do you have a team who can encourage you to take that first step?

21

Exercising Your Courage Muscles

Imagine how your life could be transformed if you stepped outside your personal comfort zone! If we reverse this logic, if you continue in the future as you have in the past, will you reach your finest hour? The clever expression, "If we always do what we have always done, we will always get what we have always gotten," still applies.

"Courage to Churchill was more than a spirited charge into a hurricane of bullets. The highest privilege was the freedom to choose; the meanest affliction was to live without options. He gave options to a world running out of time and space."

Norman Cousins

To get a different outcome in our lives means we must do something differently on the front end. The cause and effect relationship tells us that to get a different effect requires a different cause. If we are committed to achieving a new vision, we must intentionally choose to act in new or different ways.

How do we step outside our personal comfort zone? We do it with courage and with intention. There are no shortcuts or fancy psychological formulas. If creating our finest hour becomes a compelling enough vision for us, we will recognize the need to take bold steps to achieve it.

Most people stumble by attempting to take too great a step at first. When we spoke about vision, we said it was important not to eat more than we could chew. Over-stretched muscles will become damaged and prevent further exercise until they recover. The same applies to stepping outside our personal comfort zone. Initially take smaller steps, gain some successes, build some confidence, and then take larger and larger steps. Small increments of personal change will add up over time. Like compound interest, it is the long-term investment instead of the get-rich-quick scheme that we want to pursue.

Let me give some examples of stepping outside a comfort zone in each of the different dimensions of a person's life. These may sound easy because they are— when we take small steps outside our comfort zone, it is easy. Small steps still get us to our desired goal. There is nothing to fear. We think we're taking a big risk, but in reality it's only a small one!

Stepping outside your physical comfort zone (Be sure to get a doctor's concurrence, if needed!):
* If you do not exercise, begin to walk three days a week.
* If you exercise with weights, increase the amount of weights or the number of repetitions you lift.
* If you always take the same route to work, take a different route.

Stepping outside your intellectual comfort zone:
* If you only read two books a year, read one book a month.
* If you haven't taken a college course in some time, take a course at the community college or on the Internet.
* If you're not a teacher, teach a course, scout group, or discussion group.

Stepping outside your emotional comfort zone:
* If you are an emotionally private person, share your feelings with someone you love.
* If you have a quiet, reserved personality, talk to a newcomer at church, school, or other social gathering.
* If you are an outgoing, talkative person, attempt to speak with another person without using the word "I."
* If you are a forceful, decisive person, listen intently to another person.

Stepping outside your spiritual comfort zone:
* If you don't have a devotional period during the day, begin one.
* If you've never led a Bible study or Sunday school class, volunteer to lead one.

◆ If you never forget the wrongs done to you by others, practice forgiving them.

Do you get the idea? Wherever we are, we must regularly do something that we would not normally choose to do. If it makes you somewhat uncomfortable, then you are stretching your courage muscles. Remember, a person who runs the same distance each day no longer stretches his cardiovascular system and thus does not strengthen his body. The idea is to continue to stretch and thereby grow into the person who will live his or her dreams.

> *"Man's mind, once stretched by a new idea, never regains its original dimensions."*
> **Oliver Wendell Holmes, Jr.**

If we are ever going to achieve our vision, we must take that first step. Imagine trying to move a railroad car down the track. There is an incredible weight to overcome! Once the train begins to move, however, it will take less work to keep it in motion.

Overcoming our mental inertia becomes the critical step in our methodology. What does it take to overcome it? It takes courage. How do we develop courage? We do it by routinely stepping outside our behavioral comfort zones.

We must condition our bodies, our minds, and our spirits to experience change. When we are comfortable, we are not inclined to change. On the other hand, if we are to dream big dreams, we must be prepared to do something that we are currently not doing.

"Courage is resistance to fear,
mastery of fear—not absence of fear."
Mark Twain

In this section, we will work on stepping outside our comfort zones. We may be aware of the boundaries of our comfort zone, but often this represents a blind spot in our actions. We know what will stretch us, but due to fear, we choose not to expose ourselves to change.

Change is inevitable in our lives. When we orchestrate the change, we feel more comfortable with it. After all, who likes surprises? Surprisingly, we all do! Think about birthday presents or Christmas gifts. The unknown may make other surprises less welcome, but how do we know these other surprises will not be as enjoyable and full of potential as our birthday presents?

"With opportunities come responsibility.
Strength is granted to us all when we
are needed to serve in great causes."
Winston Churchill

We need a way to condition our minds to change. If we can become more acclimatized to change, our fear of it will diminish! So let's practice raising the bar and stretching our personal comfort zones.

ACTION THIS DAY

1. What can you practice this week that will cause you to step outside your physical comfort zone?

2. What can you practice this week that will cause you to step outside your intellectual comfort zone?

3. What can you practice this week that will cause you to step outside your emotional comfort zone?

4. What can you practice this week that will cause you to step outside your spiritual comfort zone?

Now that you have come up with some ways to gently stretch your courage muscles, what do you need to do? You need to practice. The ball has been passed to you, and it's up to you to run down the field. Can you do it? Yes, you can!

22

Staying the Course

Let's summarize where we have been. We shed our emotional baggage by putting the past in the past. We started with a clean, unpainted canvas on which to paint our life's dreams. We created a vision of what we wanted to be, do, or have. We needed courage to take that first step, and we found it.

So how do we make progress on our masterpiece? We need to keep painting. This brings us to the third important principle of our formula for success. The first principle we covered was vision. The second principle we studied was courage. Determination is the third principle. Determination means remaining in action until we achieve our vision.

Painting does not just require seeing the details but also seeing the big picture. The artist must see the relationship of shapes, colors, and values (light to dark), as well as have an eye for composition and perspective.

After the artist masters the basics, he can attempt to express how he feels about his subject.

"When you get right down to the root meaning of the word 'succeed,' you find that it simply means to follow through."
F. W. Nichol

What did it take for Churchill to find some stress relief from his hectic life? It took a conscious effort, first to master the basics of painting and then to paint when he needed to recharge himself. Following through gave life and reality to his vision and demanded determination.

Painting, for Churchill, became a pastime of incredible pleasure. He completed over six hundred oils (many of which never left his studio and were painted over). He liked to use bright colors. His many landscapes revealed an excellent understanding of perspective and composition. He painted thickly, that is, he used a great deal of paint, and his brushwork was readily visible.

Creating Your Finest Hour
Third Principle:
DETERMINATION
"Never give in!"

Do you see how the three principles are linked? Vision establishes what you want to be, do, or have. Courage is what is you need to get started. Determination is required to continue your actions until you achieve your vision.

"Neither the length of the struggle nor any form of severity which it may assume shall make us weary or shall make us quit."
Winston Churchill

You've now created your vision. You've taken that first step with courage. What usually happens then? People around you may attempt to blow out the candles—not just your detractors, but also your friends and maybe even your own family. They will all tell you why your vision cannot be achieved.

It won't be long before the worst critic of all shows up. Who's that? It's you! It's your own mind! Remember what they called that in the 1956 science fiction thriller, *Forbidden Planet*? "Monsters of the id." Self-doubt steals more dreams than the worst thief. We rob ourselves. As the cartoon character Pogo said, "We have met the enemy, and it's us!"

How do we resist the corroding influence of self-doubt? The key is to remain in action toward your vision. Keep your momentum going. At the same time, think back to your vision. Review in your mind the list of twenty or more reasons why you absolutely *had* to achieve your vision. Is your vision worth the sacrifice?

Of course it is! Are you willing to deal with hardships, criticism, and ridicule to achieve your vision? Of course you are! Can you do it? Of course you can!

"When faced with a mountain
I WILL NOT QUIT!
I will keep striving until I climb over,
find a pass through, tunnel underneath,
or simply stay and turn the mountain
into a gold mine, with God's help!"
Robert Schuller

ACTION THIS DAY

1. What doubts do you have about taking action toward your vision? What can you do to build confidence and assurance?

2. Supporters are great at following through. How can you use your strengths to achieve your vision?

3. What are the biggest obstacles you'll have to overcome as you pursue your vision? Who can help you deal with these obstacles?

4. Who may be your biggest detractors as you take action toward your dreams? How will you handle their criticism?

5. How can you also make your journey toward your vision a way of expressing love for those you care about?

6. There are times when others will attempt to prevent you from pursuing your dreams. They may try to make you feel guilty since you're not attending to their needs. How can you say "no" and still avoid conflict? Why is this important?

7. Imagine how it will feel when you achieve your vision: Describe the posture, facial expression, breathing, voice, gestures, and visual images you will have after you have achieved your vision. When you feel like quitting, recreate these feelings of success and press on!

PART • FIVE

Mobilizing the
English Language
(Especially for Conceptualizers)

23

A Noble Thing

Conceptualizers are detail-oriented people whose standards of accuracy and quality are extremely high. They see the world through a microscope. The rules and regulations of life and society cause these intuitive and controlled individuals to evaluate carefully all the information they can obtain. (Probably they will read this entire book, not just their designated chapters!)

Throughout Winston Churchill's long political career, he was called upon to be a master of details. Having served in almost every cabinet position in his government, he routinely read, analyzed, and produced volumes of rules and regulations concerning every facet of British life.

The generation that lived through the Second World War remembers Churchill best by his defiant speeches. His heroic words were like beacons of hope to a world in trouble. Later generations, most likely, learned about Churchill through his extensive writing.

It is amazing that a person who flunked English three times in grade school in the 1880's would later be awarded the Nobel Prize for Literature in 1953. Churchill wrote histories, biographies, memoirs, an autobiography, speeches, articles, letters, and one novel. In all, his output exceeded thirty million words!

What was the secret of his success? The difficulties that kept him repeating English (while his classmates were learning Latin and Greek) gave him abundant opportunity to master it. In his autobiography he said, "I got into my bones the essential structure of the ordinary British sentence—which is a noble thing."

Churchill's writing provides a good example of how a person takes an intellectual effort, like a book or speech, from concept formulation to finished product. The methodology is yet another example of how a person can apply the Churchill Factors to almost any aspect of life.

"Our aspirations are our possibilities."
Robert Browning

Churchill's prodigious literary output partly originated from a compelling need to earn income. He certainly had a story to tell, and he had an exceptional gift for telling it. Even before he occupied leadership positions of prominence (and writing was a means to further his political ambitions), he possessed an inner need to share his perceptions and understanding of national and international events with others. Churchill's lavish tastes and aristocratic lifestyle kept his pen active for a large part of his life.

The development of a book or a speech is similar, although the end of the process is different. A finished book is sent to editors, publishers, and publicists. A completed speech must be rehearsed and eventually cast upon an audience.

Let's start at the beginning of the process. Before any information is gathered, there must be a plan. What is the purpose of the book or speech? Who is the intended audience? In effect, what is the author's expectation or desired outcome? This is his vision.

There are several ways to develop a vision. The approach used in this book employs the analogy of a newspaper reporter writing a cover story. Churchill would have easily identified with this approach. During the Victorian wars at the turn of the twentieth century, he was one of the highest paid journalists in Britain. We can also identify with a reporter since we, the readers, want to know certain information. Typically we will look for this in the lead paragraphs and then expect to see more detailed descriptions in the body of the story.

> *"It is very important*
> *not to underrate the problem.*
> *It is also very important not to overrate it."*
> **Winston Churchill**

What information do we want to know (and expect the reporter to provide)? We desire to know who, what, when, where, why, and how. These are the questions that the reporter will seek to answer. Look at any major newspaper and notice how the reporter answers all the information the reader wants to know. We must have the same kind of dedication when we develop our vision.

Reporter's Approach:

Who? What? When?
Where? Why? How?
Written with Headline

Let's look at how each of these elements applies to the Churchill example.

Who: This refers to the person who has the vision. This can be a single person, such as you, or it can be a group of people. The group may be your team, section, department, division, or organization. The group can also be as large as your neighborhood, county, state, or nation. The "who" can be related to your professional associations or to your personal relationships. In our example, the "who" is Winston Churchill.

What: This is a detailed description of the desired outcome, expectation, or result. Remember, a vision can be a single goal that you want to accomplish. Most of the time a vision is a larger outcome that will involve achieving a number of smaller goals. The detailed descriptions of the vision provide the substance of what you desire to accomplish.

The "what" can also be referred to as a specific, measurable result. Let's first discuss "specific." "To get rich" is general. "To earn X dollars per year by working at profession Y" is specific. The more specific, that is, the more detailed, the better. Why? Without sufficient detail, there is ambiguity, and ambiguity creates inaction. In our Churchill example, a book would be too general. A history, biography, autobiography, memoirs, novel, or speech would be specific enough.

Let's now look at the second part of a specific, measurable result. We need a way to measure our progress in attaining our vision. Why? Because we need a means to tell us whether we are moving closer to our desired outcome or further away. Measurability is often called a measure of effectiveness (MOE). Without a MOE, we may not be able to gauge whether our efforts are productive or not. The MOE is a yardstick or barometer of our progress.

Vision setters can use any of the routine MOEs such as time, distance, weight, speed, dollars, or the like. They can also be more creative in devising unique MOEs to fit the desired outcome. For example, using our Churchill example, his measure might be 2,000 words per day or two chapters per month.

Measuring intangibles such as loyalty, morale, or love may require some creative thinking. Number of cars in the parking lot after normal working hours might be a measure of employee morale or loyalty. The bottom line is that the "what" in a vision has to be specific and measurable.

When: A vision without a "by when" is merely a daydream. "When" transforms a person's intentions into a promise or commitment. Open-ended activities not only tend to linger on (seemingly forever) but cause the visionary to lose his or her enthusiasm for the outcome. People tend not to commit to a vision that is ambiguous and open-ended.

By adding a deadline to our dreams, we are able to create a sense of urgency that in turn breeds excitement and enthusiasm. In the case of Churchill's writing, for example, he might establish a two-year period by which to complete a biography. A speech would be shorter term. Since it typically took Churchill six to eight hours to prepare a forty-five-minute speech, he could respond more immediately to pressing needs to inform and motivate the Members of Parliament or his fellow countrymen.

Visions may be near-term or long-term endeavors. Short-term visions may be only three-week efforts. A vision needs to be long enough for the seeds of your dreams to bear fruit. Three months would be a better lower limit than three weeks, but the same principles apply to any duration. The longer the term of the vision, the more compelling the outcome must be. Why? We need to sustain our interest and enthusiasm over a much longer period. Unless we are absolutely on fire to achieve our vision, the longer-term ones will simply die on the vine.

Where: A location or destination, where applicable, can make a vision even more specific. The richer the details of our vision, the more likely our minds will be engaged. Location is particularly important when we visualize our vision. This helps us to rehearse mentally how we hope the future will be. (For more on visualization, see Chapter 16: Eat What you Can Chew.)

Why: If the "whats" and "whens" are the meat and potatoes of our vision, the "whys" are the spices that flavor the main courses and make them tasty. The "whys" are the compelling reasons for accomplishing our vision.

The "whys" should motivate, excite, thrill, provoke, stimulate, encourage, electrify, and move you to do whatever is required to achieve that vision. If your vision doesn't inspire you; if thinking about it doesn't make your heart pound faster; if talking about it doesn't put a smile on your face and a twinkle in your eye; then are you really committed to achieving it?

How many "whys" do we need? We need as many as are necessary to achieve the effects mentioned earlier. If your vision is truly important to you, you will need at least ten compelling reasons. Twenty would be better. Fifty are great, but one hundred would be awesome! Would there be any doubt in your mind whether you would accomplish your vision if you had a hundred compelling reasons?

What do you think Churchill's reasons were for writing his six-volume, *The Second World War?* Churchill not only lived through and survived two world wars, but he also served in senior government positions that were directly responsible for the conduct of the war. He saw the folly of war, especially how the Second World War grew out of the decaying remnants of the First. Churchill was an observer of the carnage on the Western Front in World War I as well as of the Blitz on London in World War II.

> *"In War: Resolution*
> *In Defeat: Defiance*
> *In Victory: Magnanimity*
> *In Peace: Goodwill"*
> **Winston Churchill**

Churchill the statesman had his eyes focused on the distant horizon. He clearly hoped that sharing his observations of the most terrible global conflagration might keep future politicians from marching down the road to complete world annihilation.

How: "How" defines the action steps that are necessary to achieve our vision. These action steps are also bound by specific periods of time to complete the action. A plan of action with milestones (POA & M) has long been used as a management tool to track significant projects. Basically, the vision is broken down into its component steps. This is equivalent to outlining a book first by chapter, and then, if necessary, page by page.

The old adage, "How do you eat an elephant? You do it one bite at a time," still applies. People do better when the food they chew is bite-size. Vision, like food, is best digested in a reasonable way. How many organizations in corporate America, or even in the federal government, failed to achieve their vision because of their psychological gluttony?

Too ambitious a vision can often spell disaster for an organization. A vision needs to be commensurate with the talents, creativity, and energies of those who are to make the vision happen. A CEO who sets the high-jump bar at seven feet when his best jumpers can barely clear five feet may be setting the organization up for failure, disappointment, and loss of corporate esteem.

> ## *"How far, alas, do man's endeavors fall short in practice of his aspirations!"*
> **Winston Churchill**

While it is true that most people underestimate their abilities and potential, it is more prudent to walk before you run. A person or an organization needs to be conditioned for success. Afterward, they can set and achieve progressively more difficult, demanding, and complex visions.

The "how" gives life to the vision. It takes the outcome and breaks it down into more achievable action steps. In the case of writing a speech, Churchill would jot down some main points or themes he wished to convey.

He would do some research to gather the facts and figures that supported his points. He would then develop the speech, having his secretaries copy down his dictation. After the speech was transcribed, he would edit and revise it. The speech would then be typed in Churchill's "psalm form" and practiced (sometimes while Churchill was in the bath tub!). Even though Churchill had an extraordinary memory, he always had a copy of his speech available whenever he spoke. (This was the result of having his mind go blank once during a speech early in his political career.) The vision became real when he stood before the House of Commons and lifted his voice into history.

"Never in the field of human conflict was so much owed by so many to so few."
Winston Churchill

Written: What is needed to make our vision complete? It must be written. Putting our vision on paper makes it a tangible record to which we can refer as we proceed to the finish line.

Conceptualizers are the kind of people who take the time to paint their masterpiece on the canvas with great accuracy. They mix their colors with care. They use small, distinct brushstrokes to capture every detail. They don't want to overlook anything, so they always follow the rules about color, composition, and tone. With fortitude and with well-thought-out reasoning they paint their masterpieces.

Headline: Only one thing remains before our reporter can move on to the next activity. He must develop a catchy title for his article—one which will attract readers. This headline becomes his vision statement. A vision statement can be one sentence or many pages in length. The shorter, more concise it is, the easier we can memorize and internalize it. For our example of Churchill's six-volume *The Second World War*, a vision statement might be, "Former Prime Minister seeks to promote world peace by documenting his observations of the Second World War."

Creating Your Finest Hour
First Principle:

VISION

"If you can see it, you can paint it!"

Let's now look at some questions that may help you develop a vision that you would like to achieve. This is the beginning of the approach that will help you to create your finest hour.

ACTION THIS DAY

1. Considering your dreams for the future, what is the most you think you can achieve professionally? Can you actually accomplish more than you think you can?

2. Conceptualizers are often intuitive. Have you ever made intuitive instead of fact-based decisions? What was the result?

3. In dealing with other people, what is your biggest frustration? What do you think is their biggest frustration in dealing with you? Why?

4. What has your insistence on precision, accuracy, and quality of work performance cost you? Would your life be more fulfilling or satisfying by changing (for example, relaxing) any of your standards?

5. Whom could you enlist to help you achieve your vision? With whom would you celebrate when you achieve your vision?

6. How would you like to be remembered by a friend who was asked to write your obituary?

Now that you have thought about some of the areas that define who you are, let's take this opportunity and develop a vision based on the questions used by reporters when they cover a story. Select something that you would like to accomplish within the next four months. Using a blank sheet of paper, write the answers to the seven questions.

1. Who?

2. What? (Specific and measurable.)

3. When? (When you will achieve your outcome.)

4. Where?

5. Why? (List the compelling reasons why you absolutely must accomplish your vision. How about 10 reasons?)

6. How? (List some of the key action steps you will have to take to accomplish your vision.)

7. Vision statement. (Now you have written all of the elements of your vision. What headline will you give it?)

24

Opening Opportunity's Door

"Remember the story of the Spanish prisoner. For many years he was confined in a dungeon....One day it occurred to him to push the door of his cell. It was open; and it had never been locked."
Winston Churchill

What happens when Conceptualizers do not have enough information to make a decision? They may tend to defer a decision until they can obtain the needed information. Can this reluctance have an impact on their ability to create their finest hour? Let's consider the possibilities.

Because of its life-or-death outcome, one of the best proving grounds for decision making has been in war. War tends to accelerate the decision-making process as well as produce the maximum amount of stress on the decision makers.

In war, decisions are made that may significantly impact the lives and fortunes of others. Although time is the same for all adversaries, those who can act or react quickest using the data at hand tend to be the victors. Courage is the catalyst that enables them to act. (The western gunfight adage about "the quick and the dead" really is valid.)

Consider the impact of surprise in warfare. History is replete with examples where the element of surprise allowed an inferior force to defeat a larger, better-equipped, better-trained one. Once again, courage means taking action without having all the information.

In war, the requirement to take extreme measures is necessary to ensure survival. How about in our professional or personal lives? Do our lives have to be threatened in order to act without abundant information? What would be the impact on our future if we took calculated risks even though our lives were not being threatened?

*"All life involves the
management of risk, not its elimination."*
Walter Wriston

Any time people communicate, there is risk. There is the risk that one person will misunderstand the other. One person may simply see the world from a different viewpoint than the other. One party may be visual and the other auditory. The possibility of risks should not deter us from action. All the desired information will rarely be available at the time a decision must be made. This means that we must decide how important is it to act versus how important is it to wait until we have "all" the information needed to decide.

"When you come to a fork in the road, take it."
Yogi Berra

How high is up? How much is enough? Vision itself is nothing until a person takes that first step. Faith in the most elaborate, well-conceived plan without any action is like a giant oak tree that has withstood the ravages of time. The tree's sturdy but twisted limbs and broad trunk were a symbol of ageless strength. One night, however, lightning struck the oak and split it open. The next morning people from all over saw that the oak was but a hollow shell. The inner part of the tree had been gutted by decay. Will you let your vision—that derives its creation from the essence of who you are—decay from the inside out because you never took that first courageous step toward victory?

"The maxim, 'Nothing avails but perfection,' spells paralysis."
Winston Churchill

Winston Churchill's writing career would never have changed the lives of millions if he had chosen to wait until his books were perfect. To be perfect means to be complete; nothing else needs to be added. There can always be another source to check or another reference to correlate the facts. Instead, Churchill found the appropriate balance between presenting just what was necessary to educate and enlighten the reader without overwhelming him with unnecessary facts.

> *"You have to run risks. There are no certainties in war. There is a precipice on either side of you—the precipice of caution and the precipice of over-daring."*
> **Winston Churchill**

If we are prone to defer our decisions to reduce our risks, we may find ourselves mired in tar pits like the dinosaurs. Those great beasts got stuck in the thick, black ooze and died because they couldn't move. Will our visions die a slow, frustrating death because they become stuck in the tar pits of inaction?

Creating Your Finest Hour
Second Principle:

COURAGE

"Do it now, and don't look back!"

The boldest military leaders trained their men to run toward the sound of gunfire, for that's where the enemy was. Today, we ought to run toward our vision, for that is where our finest hour will be found.

To run toward our vision may be an understatement. If we have enough compelling reasons why we must accomplish our vision, we will be accelerating at warp speed! If we aren't, perhaps we're not truly committed to our vision.

> *"Don't concentrate on risks. Concentrate on results. No risk is too great to prevent the necessary job from getting done."*
> **Chuck Yeager**

Risk management means that we consider all the information available at the time, weigh the options, select the best option, and act in some way. Shouldn't we check to see if opportunity's door is locked? Maybe it has been open all the time!

ACTION THIS DAY

1. What is the greatest fear you have as you pursue your vision? Why? What steps can you take to overcome this fear?

2. How do you react to criticism of your work? How do others tend to disagree with you? Can you see their point of view? Could they be right?

3. How would you diplomatically explain to someone how to balance perfectionism and timely action? What are the dangers of being a perfectionist?

4. There are details, and there are critical details. How can you tell the difference between the two as you pursue your vision?

5. Can you ever really have enough information to reach a decision? Why? How much more could you accomplish if you learned to reach a decision with half as much information? Are you willing to experiment and analyze the success rate of the decisions you make using less information?

6. How do you adapt to change or to areas that do not have any established guidelines, rules, or regulations? How can you make change work for you?

25

The Greatest Dictator of All Time

The midnight quiet of the country mansion was only broken by the deliberate cadence of muffled footsteps and the resonant, measured voice of a man who transformed words into magical expressions of confidence and resolve. What a Stradivarius is to violins or a G. Loomis to fly-fishing rods, Churchill is to oratory. His heroic exclamations, exhortations, and quips are legend. Churchill, Shakespeare, Mark Twain, and the Bible account for perhaps three-quarters of the quotations used by public speakers.

> *"Churchill mobilized the English*
> *language and sent it into battle."*
> **Edward R. Murrow**

Like everything else about Churchill, his writing habits were unique. Churchill did his own background research for each speech, newspaper article, or magazine piece. Oxford graduate students and former military officers augmented his research for some of his larger works. They provided him with an array of facts and figures. From this, Churchill refined the ore in the blast furnace of his mind. He separated out the impurities and discarded them in the slag heap. The remaining pure metal was ready to be poured into a cast. Many of his researchers marveled at his prescient ability to discern the key issues or trends from the information provided. More than once his assistants found only small nuggets while sifting through background material. On the other hand, Churchill would often strike a rich vein while reviewing the same information!

Churchill preferred to write his books and articles by dictating them. He paced the floor of his study like a lion reflecting on the prey it would soon consume. Fresh from an evening of fine food, fine company, and fine conversation (mostly his own), Churchill would begin work about eleven in the evening and continue until two to four o'clock in the morning. His pace of dictation began slowly, like a gentle spring. He groped for the right word. Soon the spring became a bubbling brook, then a gathering stream, then a raging river, and then a thundering ocean of power and majesty.

Churchill developed his habit of dictation as a teenage student at Harrow. He refined the technique to the point where he typically required a battery of secretaries to record his prolific dictation. One secretary would spend thirty minutes or more "before the Churchillian mast." Then a "fresh" secretary was needed to capture the cannonade of words. The secretary who was relieved would then type up the draft for Churchill to edit later. More than one new secretary reported that her "baptism under fire" was a terrifying experience.

Few men have achieved Churchill's impressive and prodigious output of words. Churchill's son Randolph borrowed John Lockhart's words when he began the official biography of his famous father by writing, "He shall be his own biographer." On a good night Churchill may have dictated five thousand words. His lifetime productivity of over thirty million words proved his son's assertion. With today's voice recognition software and fast personal computers, one can only imagine how much more Churchill could have produced!

> *"Short words are best, and old words when short are the best of all."*
> **Winston Churchill**

Churchill's defiant speeches in 1940 and 1941, while Britain stood alone against Hitler's Germany, rallied his countrymen and encouraged the hearts of free people everywhere. His command of the English language was only exceeded by the scope of his historical perspective. His speeches were built around simple words. (In a similar way, the brushstrokes on his landscape paintings suggested, rather than detailed, his impressions of a scene.) He skillfully wove word pictures with a dramatic sense of urgency. His use of emotion gave a personal dimension to his fact-laden speeches. He kept the listener's attention by focusing on only one theme in each speech. With his words, he resonated the sentiments of his audience and stirred them on to action.

Since Churchill dictated most of his speeches and books, you can capture the full grandeur of his writing by listening to, rather than reading, his works. Churchill's speeches, in his own voice, give the best means of hearing the power of his heroic rhetoric. In addition, Books On Tape, Inc., has a large unabridged selection of Churchill's books on audiocassette. (See Appendix II.) These audiobooks are all read by professional voices and offer the listener the opportunity to hear the lordly style of one of the greatest masters of the English language.

Churchill's repeated use of the written and spoken word reveals the third element in our methodology.

Creating Your Finest Hour
Third Principle:
DETERMINATION
"Never give in!"

Determination implies that once we establish a vision, we must continue to move forward until we achieve our desired outcome. Is there any other way? In our professional and personal lives, there are no real substitutes for good old-fashioned perseverance. The ability to remain focused on our vision and take whatever measures are necessary for its achievement becomes a highly-prized character trait.

"You may have to fight a battle more than once to win it."
Margaret Thatcher

Patience is one of the key ingredients that will allow determination to thrive. Things rarely happen as quickly as we desire. The Japanese, long known for their patient natures, sought to teach their children patience with origami (paper folding). The patient person who confidently moves forward will ultimately be rewarded for his actions.

When the quality movement (originally made in America) was exported back from Japan in the 1970's, American businesses were exposed to the concept of continuous quality improvement. In particular, continuous improvement involved optimizing the different processes in a business. By eliminating variance in the finished products or services, businesses could develop products that better satisfied the needs of the user.

"The stronger your imagination the more variegated your universe."
Winston Churchill

Unfortunately senior management was often reluctant to embrace continuous improvement that involved five-, ten-, or twenty-year timelines. (Small improvements, however, over a long period can result in significant benefits.) They fell back to the quarterly projections they were used to instead of taking the long-term perspective of excellence. Small incremental improvements simply were not as flashy as quantum-level improvements in performance. They sought breakthrough performance and its dramatic results, not realizing that a completely different corporate culture was required for breakthroughs. Such a culture is based on "possibility" and the power of the individual or team to "invent an extraordinary future and live into it." This requires a much higher level of commitment and personal relationships than one finds in the continuous improvement approach.

"We shall go forward together. The road upward is stony. There are upon our journey dark and dangerous valleys through which we have to make and fight our way. But it is sure and certain that if we persevere—and we shall persevere—we shall come through these dark and dangerous valleys into the sunlight broader and more genial and more lasting than mankind has ever known."

Winston Churchill

Which methodology yields better results: continuous improvement or breakthrough performance? The answer lies in what the personal or business vision may be. Both approaches may produce the desired results. Compound interest over time may be much safer than Internet trading of stocks. One must balance the degree of risk versus time to determine which approach is more acceptable. Patience and perseverance, however, remain virtues in either approach.

ACTION THIS DAY

1. What are the greatest impediments or obstacles preventing you from achieving your vision?

2. How will you motivate yourself to remain committed to your vision? Do you have any rituals or habits that have proved successful in the past?

3. What new standards of performance, accuracy, or quality will you need in order to be more successful at achieving your vision?

4. Do you practice continuous improvement in your professional life? Can you export any of the techniques or philosophies you use professionally to your personal life, or vice versa? If so, which ones?

5. Do you tend to overprepare for every contingency? What is the cost of doing this? How can you gauge the most likely results better and thus spend less time preparing for unlikely scenarios?

26

It Really Takes A Team

Conceptualizers prefer to work alone. This practice, however, can be extremely limiting. The reason lies in the way we create or innovate.

Each person has an awareness of countless subjects, many of which might be at the authority or expert level. For example, Churchill was certainly knowledgeable about a vast array of subjects including British politics, European history, military technology, landscape oil painting, and the like.

> *"Imagination, without deep and full knowledge, is a snare."*
> **Winston Churchill**

Each person has an awareness that there are even more subjects about which he has little or no knowledge.

Churchill knew little about quantum mechanics, brain surgery, American baseball, or Chinese cooking.

This awareness of what we know and what we do not know constitutes the usual database a person can access when confronted with a problem or challenge. There is, however, another domain that can greatly expand a person's menu of options. This area lies completely outside a person's awareness. In other words, a person does not know that he does not know! Mining into this rich deposit of ore can indeed produce a mother lode of possibilities.

> *"Some men see things as they are,*
> *and say, 'Why?' I dream of things*
> *that never were, and say, 'Why not?'"*
> **George Bernard Shaw**

This "what you didn't know that you didn't know" region is the fountainhead of innovation, growth, new possibilities, extraordinary futures, and breakthroughs! If a person were able to tap into this region, he or she would be exposed to new knowledge that lies outside his or her awareness. So how does one discover this field of dreams? Actually the answer is surprisingly simple.

To access information that is outside your personal awareness, simply speak with another person! For example, Churchill knew that the science of radio propagation existed, but he knew essentially nothing about it. By discussing the subject with his friend, Professor Frederick Lindemann, Churchill was able to grasp the importance of using it to deceive and confuse German bombers. Thus, because of the consultations of two leaders, many Nazi bombs fell harmlessly in empty fields instead of in heavily populated areas.

Conceptualizers can vastly expand the possibilities of their own minds simply by speaking with other people. This is why a team of committed individuals, each bringing his own awareness of knowledge, talents, and experiences, represents a more powerful resource than that of a single person.

"We must all drive ourselves to the utmost limit of our strength. We must preserve and refine our sense of proportion. We must strive to combine the virtues of wisdom and of daring. We must move forward together, united and inexorable."
Winston Churchill

In addition to expanding the domains of awareness, by including the mindset of Drivers, Influencers, and Supporters, Conceptualizers would gain a completely different view of the world. Drivers would offer new possibilities involving direct, decisive, and risk-taking options especially when challenges or change were present. Influencers would provide new possibilities involving optimistic, participatory, or entertaining options. These in turn would expand geometrically due to one Influencer's proclivity to involve many others. Finally, Supporters would give new possibilities involving relational, nurturing, practical, and methodical options.

Conceptualizers need not play John Wayne and source the solutions to challenges and problems all by themselves. By speaking with others, they can greatly expand the possible options that lie outside their own personal awareness. (Actually, all four behavioral styles would benefit from the viewpoint, knowledge, talents, and experiences of others.)

It was not long ago when corporations sought to clone their employees to be the same. They were encouraged to dress alike, behave alike, and even think alike. In today's global marketplace, being the same will hasten the trip to the corporate undertaker. The pace of change, technology, economics, government regulations, information, and the like demands new, innovative solutions. If the principal decision makers in an organization all think alike, then most of them are redundant!

Diversity is the key to survival in today's global arena. A diversity of behavioral styles, leadership styles, innovation styles, knowledge, talents, experiences, and demographic backgrounds, will allow an organization to consider a challenge or problem from many different viewpoints. As a result, the diverse team will be able to propose many more solutions than the non-diverse organization. More solutions give the decision makers additional options to consider and, therefore, enhance their likelihood not just of survival but of success!

ACTION THIS DAY

1. What concerns you most about discussing your challenges and problems with others?

2. Who are some Drivers with whom you can discuss your challenges or problems? What qualities and points of view will they give you that you don't have?

3. Who are some Influencers with whom you can discuss your challenges or problems? What qualities and points of view will they give you that you don't have?

4. Who are some Supporters with whom you can discuss your challenges or problems? What qualities and points of view will they give you that you don't have?

5. Who are some other Conceptualizers with whom you can discuss your challenges or problems? What qualities and points of view will they give you that you don't have?

6. Why is your point of view valuable to Drivers, Influencers, Supporters, and other Conceptualizers? Are there opportunities where you now might want to share your expertise?

PART • SIX

Applying the Churchill Factors

27

Completing Your Masterpiece

Look at your masterpiece, that is, at you. As you continue to work to improve your professional or personal life, you know you have a proven, reliable methodology that serves as a roadmap. We have developed simple principles that will help us harness hope and can serve as a means to help us create our finest hour. The Churchill Factors are simple, but not easy. They are simple to understand, but their application requires intention, discipline, and dedication.

> *"There are no great men, only great challenges, that ordinary men are forced by circumstances to meet."*
> **William F. Halsey**

Most people look at a towering leader like Sir Winston Churchill and see a life full of extraordinary achievements. Few, however, realize that his road to greatness was neither straight nor smooth. He had to wage a constant battle with setbacks, trials, defeats and even depression. His ability to turn adversity into advantage can be traced to his simple formula of success that he practiced throughout his life. Using the Churchill Factors, you too can create your finest hour!

The Churchill Factors

VISION
"If we can see it, we can paint it!"

COURAGE
"Do it now, and don't look back!"

DETERMINATION
"Never give in!"

When can we use this methodology? We can use it whenever we choose. We can use it to play the most important game of our lives. We can use it when we are by ourselves. We can use it when we are on a team. We can use it when we enter into a new relationship or when we want to improve an old one. We can use it when we become a new parent.

We can use it all the time! We can use it to achieve large dreams or small ones. We can use it when we begin a new project or start a new job. We can use it when we assume a new leadership responsibility, either in our professional or personal lives. In all of these applications, the three principles deal with these questions:

1. What do I want to be, do, or have?

2. What do I need to do to get started?

3. What do I need to do to achieve my outcome?

During our discussion of developing our vision using the reporter's questions, we spoke about making the "what" measurable. Having some yardstick will help us track our progress. Are our actions getting us closer to our vision or further away? We can refine our actions to help us hit the target.

What if we establish a vision, take that first step with courage, press on boldly toward our desired outcome, and then discover we've aimed at the wrong target? Should we continue on with determination? No! We have free choice! If we find that we have made errors in our original vision, perhaps due to faulty assumptions or lack of accurate information, we simply return to the vision stage and start over again. This methodology is intended to be iterative, that is, it can be refined as many times as necessary until you achieve the desired results.

If we add an element of fun into the game, we'll enjoy the process all the more. Reinventing your life should be fun. Why shouldn't we experience satisfaction, joy, and fulfillment? We can achieve our heart's desire and be a role model for others. We can run the good race and finish with a flourish.

There is a tendency among some people to be content wherever they are. Comfort breeds complacency. They do not want to rock the boat. They will readily give in to others, particularly in satisfying the needs of others before their own. These, of course, are all choices.

At some point, if a person wants to move forward, he will have to focus himself and step outside his personal comfort zone. It may be trite, but it's still true: "the turtle goes nowhere until he sticks out his neck."

"By our courage, our endurance, and our brains, we have made our way in the world to the lasting benefit of mankind. Let us not lose heart. Our future is one of high hope."
Winston Churchill

If being comfortable keeps us from moving toward our vision, then distractions act to throw us off course. If a helmsman on a ship were distracted, he'd probably miss his next port of call. Don't distractions take us off course at home, at work, and in every facet of our lives?

Distractions affect Drivers, Influencers, Supporters, and Conceptualizers differently. Drivers, who are single-minded and task-oriented, prefer to focus on the bottom line. Hence, they tend to be distracted by small things. This especially applies to details that don't seem to relate to the bottom-line mission with which they are involved. When they devote time to these distractions, they lose focus on their bottom-line, big-picture tasks.

Influencers are susceptible to being distracted by other activities that offer an element of fun. Since they have a people-oriented focus and look for fun in their work, they can easily be sidetracked by other entertaining diversions.

"The mark of a person is not how well they do what they like to do, but rather how well they do what they do not like to do."
Richard Nixon

Supporters feel a need to help other people. Regardless of what they are doing, if someone comes to them with a need, they will divert their focus from their original vision and lend their assistance, even to tangential or unimportant jobs..

Finally, Conceptualizers are distracted when too many details are involved. The discovery of new information will prevent them from completing a project. They will not want to move forward until they have studied and evaluated all the new details.

What is the remedy for "distractionitis?" It is discipline! Discipline means we resist distractions and remain focused on the task being pursued. Discipline is an active, not a passive sport. Each of us must be aware of the unique kinds of distractions we are susceptible to and then exercise discipline to remain focused on our vision. Churchill was known for his ability to focus like a laser beam on a specific project and then concentrate all his energies on it. His prolific output of written and spoken words while at the same time occupying governmental positions of great responsibility is a witness to his extraordinary powers of concentration. Discipline, then, will keep us on course to our finest hour.

> *"Forward then. Forward! Let us go forward without fear into the future and let us dread naught when duty calls."*
> **Winston Churchill**

We have spoken earlier about our capacity to be more than we ever imagined being. Each of us possesses all the innate talents to lead a joyful, productive, successful life. We must be motivated to step outside our comfort zones because being comfortable makes us complacent. There are three relentless gate guards who stand watch outside the door of fulfillment and achievement. These are:

1. **Failure of imagination**
2. **Failure of will**
3. **Failure to use time effectively**

Using the Churchill Factors enables us to overcome the first two gate guards. Failure of imagination is a lack of vision. Similarly, failure of will is a lack of courage and determination. The Churchill Factors help us transform our dreams into actions.

As we give life to our vision, we must be aware of that third gate guard. Failure to use our time effectively can prevent the fulfillment of our vision.

Time is the greatest common denominator for all of us. We are all blessed with twenty-four hours each day. Billy Graham, Bill Gates, and Bill Cosby have the same amount of time allotted for use each day that we do. How well we use it will determine how much we can accomplish. In the game of life there are no time-outs: the clock always keeps running! Time is life! We must take the time to be, do, and have the things that are vital to who we are as human beings. We must seize the moment and tell those who matter most to us how much we love them. There is no time to lose!

"Somebody should tell us, right at the start of our lives, that we are dying. Then we might live life to the limit, every minute of every day. There are only so many tomorrows."
Michael Landon

We have both the capacity and ability to do more with our lives. Humans are extremely adaptable and resilient beings. That most of us fail to use more than a fraction of our potential means that our families, our neighborhoods, our states, our nations, and our planet are not benefiting from all we can be, do, or have. Imagine the impact of people everywhere pushing outside their current envelope of behavior! War, hunger, poverty, prejudice, and pollution might be immeasurably decreased! Are you willing to take the risk and participate in this great endeavor? This could be your finest hour!

ACTION THIS DAY

1. How can you use the Churchill Factors in your professional life? How can you use the Churchill Factors in your personal life?

2. Now that you have the methodology, what will be the consequences of not using it?

3. In what ways will you benefit when you use the methodology?

4. Which of the three factors, vision, courage, and determination, will be most difficult for you? Why?

5. How do you need to stretch out of your comfort zone to master this difficult factor?

6. Who is available to coach or mentor you in this factor? How will you be accountable to him/her?

7. What empowering self-talk will you use to motivate yourself as you make progress toward your vision?

8. What kinds of distractions tend to pull you off course? What specific actions will you take to develop the discipline needed to resist these distractions?

9. How will you celebrate your success of achieving or making significant progress toward your vision?

10. When you have successfully achieved this vision, what will be your next vision that will take you another step closer to your finest hour?

28

Being True To Self

"Our future is in our hands.
Our lives are what we choose to make them."
Winston Churchill

The Churchill Factors give you a methodology to transform your life in the way you desire. As you paint your masterpiece on the canvas of life, never forget that everyone's masterpiece is precious, unique, and individual. Don't try to imitate someone else's masterpiece! Why? Because among over six billion humans on this planet, there is only one of you! No other human being possesses exactly the same genetic traits, personality, behavioral strengths, attitudes, values, beliefs, and experiences that you do.

Be yourself! Be true to yourself! Also remember that because you have free choice, your future does not have to come from your past. You can blaze that new trail!

"Our future rests on one foundation and only one—the courage, skill, enterprise, and ingenuity of our people. But we need more than just our native wit and intelligence. We need trained minds."
Winston Churchill

Your masterpiece is not exactly like a painting. Your masterpiece is a living masterpiece. It is never complete. It is constantly being reworked, modified, and improved. When you use vision, courage, and determination and continuously improve your masterpiece, you will experience more joy, satisfaction, and confidence in your life. As you experience new successes, you will discover that the process replicates itself. Each new success will lead to others.

"We kept on doing our best, we kept on improving. We profited by our mistakes and our experiences. We turned misfortune to good account."
Winston Churchill

As you apply the Churchill Factors, you may need some help mastering vision, courage, or determination. Think about Olympic athletes, who are the best at what they do. Two traits common to them stand out. First, although they are the best, they still practice to be a little better. There are three steps in this process: practice,

practice, and more practice! They can move faster, be more graceful, set a new performance record, or the like. Olympic athletes are all believers in continuous improvement.

The second common trait these athletes share is that even though they are the best, they have coaches to help them improve still further. They have performance coaches, nutrition coaches, psychological coaches, sports medicine coaches, etc. Who are your coaches? We all need coaches in our lives. Aren't all of us in the Olympics of our lives?

Remember, we shall never stop,
never weary, and never give in."
Winston Churchill

Who would make a good coach for you? Start with the people around you: your spouse, a parent, a grandparent, a supervisor at work, a co-worker, a friend, a pastor, a role model in your career field, a mentor, or a professional coach. If we want to push the envelope in our lives and create our finest hour, coaches can help.

In addition to coaches, each of us needs a few friends to serve as a support group, brain trust, or mastermind. We were not meant to travel through life alone, but rather to exist in a community of fellow travelers. We need the encouragement, support, and yes, the love, of others.

Don't forget also to celebrate your successes when they occur, because you earned them. Generously share the benefits of your success with others. Your words of encouragement to strangers, for example, may be the only encouragement they have ever received. Invest your humanity by being the kind of person who uses vision, courage, and determination to make a difference on this planet. You can do this by the positive example of your words and your deeds. You never know who will see in you an inner strength that will give them a source of hope.

> *"Let us go forward together and put*
> *the great principles we support to the proof."*
> **Winston Churchill**

By using the Churchill Factors, you will be identifying yourself as a leader. You will be using the same motivating desire that enabled a frail boy with a lisp, poor performance in school, and unloving parents to exceed the expectations of everyone! In the end, after all has been said and done, all that genuinely remains behind when we depart this physical world will be our example as a man or woman and the legacy of leadership we gave to others.

29

Onward to Victory

We do not have to be a towering international figure like Winston Churchill in order to use his wisdom. Regardless of the circumstances we have in our lives, we all need a method that will consistently help us realize our dreams.

The Churchill Factors are the key tools to this approach. Vision, courage, and determination open the door to a richer, fuller, more productive life. With these simple tools, you can now conquer the challenges in your life.

"Make each day's practice a masterpiece."
John Wooden

Some final thoughts are now appropriate. Vision, courage, and determination are not effective independent of each other. The three synergize and create new possibilities that will, over time, create your finest hour.

Vision without courage and determination leads to hopelessness—you can see it, but you don't believe you can get to it! Courage without vision and determination leads to tilting at windmills, taking on too many tasks and challenges that lead nowhere. Finally, determination without vision and courage makes us rigid, dogmatic, and more likely to place the blame for our lack of progress on others.

"If the human race wishes to have a prolonged and indefinite period of material prosperity, they have only got to behave in a peaceful and helpful way towards one another, and science will do for them all that they wish and more than they can dream....Nothing is final. Change is unceasing and it is likely that mankind has a lot more to learn before it comes to its journey's end....We might even find ourselves in a few years moving along a smooth causeway of peace and plenty instead of roaming around on the rim of Hell.... Thus we may by patience, courage, and in orderly progression reach the shelter of a calmer and kindlier age."

Winston Churchill

Early in the Second World War, Churchill appealed in writing to President Roosevelt for military equipment to help Britain continue its fight for freedom. At the time Britain was the only thing standing between Nazi Germany and the free world. If Britain fell, it's possible Hitler would have dominated the entire world, including the United States. During this critical time, Churchill ended his letter to the American president with these words: "Give us the tools, and we will finish the job!"

My loyal readers, you have been given the tools. It is now up to you to finish the job. If you can see it, you can paint it! Do it now and don't look back! And never, never give in! These timeless truths are as valid today for you as they were for Winston Churchill. Using the Churchill Factors will enable you to create your finest hour.

So what will vision, courage, and determination give you? Let me sum it up in one word: **VICTORY!** They'll give you victory! May your lives be victorious!

"You ask: 'What is our aim?' I can answer in one word: It is victory, victory at all costs, victory in spite of all terror, victory however long and hard the road may be; for without victory there is no survival."

Winston Churchill

"God bless you all. This is your victory!"
Winston Churchill

APPENDIX I

Advanced Applications of the Churchill Factors

We have just looked at the Churchill Factors through the eyes of each of the four behavioral styles. The purpose in each of the behavioral sections was to help the reader understand vision, courage, and determination in the context of his own lifestyle and in his own language. The questions in each of the different sections were designed to address issues that apply best to those behavioral styles.

We will discuss three levels of applications in this appendix. The first involves the amount of information needed by each of the four behavioral styles. Influencers desire the least amount of information. They primarily want the big picture and information that is people oriented. Drivers also want the big picture, but with a greater emphasis on mission-oriented, bottom-line information. Supporters want more information than Influencers or Drivers, since they want the knowledge to accomplish a task step by step. Finally, Conceptualizers desire the greatest amount of information, which they feel they need in order to reach a decision.

Thus, if you are a Driver or an Influencer and feel you need more information concerning how to create a compelling vision, build courage, or follow through with determination, you should read the sections written specifically for Supporters and Conceptualizers. In addition, there are additional subjects (for example, overcoming procrastination) in each of the sections that are not found in the other sections. Because these may also be of importance to you, a list of topics discussed in each section is summarized below:

PART TWO: In the Wilderness (For Drivers)

Bottom-Line Approach
Mission Oriented
Boldness
Meeting Challenges
Overcoming Adversity

PART THREE: A Grand Alliance (For Influencers)

Big Picture Approach
People Oriented
Collaboration
Vulnerability
Overcoming Procrastination

PART FOUR: The Landscape of Leadership (For Supporters)

Step-By-Step Approach
Relational and Encouraging
Stretching Goals
Visualizing and Paradigm Shifting
Building Courage

PART FIVE: Mobilizing the English Language (For Conceptualizers)

Most Detailed Description
Precision and Accuracy
Independent Action
Risk Taking
Working with Teams

If you did not get enough explanation in your particular section, I suggest that you read one of the other sections to gain the level of detail you require. Remember, each of us has some of each of the four behavioral dimensions. For example, an individual may be high in both the Driver and Conceptualizer traits. This kind of individual may be direct, decisive, somewhat detail-oriented, accurate, and have high standards of performance.

The second level of application builds from the first application and involves developing an awareness for the behavioral preferences of others. Although we all have some of the four dimensions of behavior, we tend to be strongest in only one or two of these. We have a preferred style that defines our personal comfort zone.

Before we can learn how to adapt our behavioral style to be more responsive to a particular situation, we must understand the other styles. The four dimensions are essentially divided equally across the population. Approximately one-fourth of the population shares a person's principal behavioral style. That means three-fourths does not!

If a person exhibits strong Conceptualizer behavior, then he will be able to establish rapport and understand other Conceptualizers fairly well. Conceptualizers see the world in basically the same way. In a behavioral sense, one person's brain is saying, "He's just like I am. Must be a good guy!" Please realize that understanding does not imply compatibility, either professionally or socially. Two Influencers, for example, will see the world similarly but will compete for the limelight at work.

If we can get along best with the quarter of the population who shares our strongest behavioral dimension, we have some work to do in order to get along with the rest! The first step is to understand something about them. There were brief descriptions in Chapter 5 of all four styles. These were thumbnail sketches intended to help each person identify his preferred style. Each of the four different sections in the book was written to illuminate the motivations, needs, concerns, and fears of each style. Furthermore, the questions in each section were customized for each of the different styles.

This all suggests that if a person wants to be more responsive to the other styles, relate better, or establish rapport faster, there is a need to understand the context or background that each style uses. Therefore, a person may choose to read all four sections. Besides getting a better understanding of how to incorporate vision, courage, and determination in his own life, he will now understand the basic assumptions of each of the styles. This leads us to the third level of application.

"The destiny of mankind is not decided by material computation. When great causes are on the move in the world, stirring all men's souls, drawing them from their firesides, casting aside comfort, wealth, and the pursuit of happiness in response to impulses at once awe-striking and irresistible, we learn that we are spirits, not animals, and that something is going on in space and time, which, whether we like it or not, spells duty."

Winston Churchill

In our daily existence we are surrounded by people: family, friends, co-workers, customers, suppliers, and strangers. How well we get along with these people is our choice. Since you are reading this book, you probably desire to enhance your interactions with other people. Think about the payoffs. At home, if you were able to get along better with your family, there might be more happiness, less stress, and better relationships. At work, there could be more harmony and cooperation, more productivity, fewer misunderstandings, and greater opportunities for promotion. In social associations, there might be a greater opportunity to make a difference in another person's life. Aren't these benefits worth the time it may take to master some relatively simple principles involving the different behavioral styles?

How does a person interact better with someone else? The simplest explanation is that the two parties must be able to communicate on common ground. Imagine a radio station broadcasting on a specific center frequency. If a person had a radio tuned to this exact frequency, he would hear every voice with perfect clarity and every sound with perfect fidelity. Now if the radio were tuned just a little off the center frequency, he would hear some distortion when listening to voices, and the music would fade in and out. Finally, if the radio were tuned far away from the radio station's center frequency, then he would hear background, noise, static, or nothing at all.

If two people are not on the same center frequency, there will be some level of distortion. In simplest terms, this means a Driver can speak with another Driver with less distortion since they share some of the same behavioral points of view. On the other hand, a Driver and a Conceptualizer would experience more distortion in their communications because they have more differences in their basic assumptions about life. Reducing the differences in points of view between two speakers would result in clearer, less distorted communications. Less distortion translates into fewer misunderstandings, less conflict, and less frustration.

What does it take for two people to get on the same wavelength? If both are familiar with the different behavioral styles, they can more readily adapt to each other. The more common scenario, however, is that only one of the two will be aware of the styles. In order to communicate on the other person's center frequency, you must adapt to the other person. Regardless of which preferred style you have, you must stretch yourself to the other person's style if you desire to enhance your communication with him.

STRETCHING YOUR STYLE

Whether you are a
Driver, Influencer, Supporter, or Conceptualizer:

In order to communicate more effectively, you must stretch out of YOUR behavioral comfort zone and adapt to the style of the OTHER person!

Consider this example. A Conceptualizer (who has read *The Churchill Factors*) is speaking with his boss (an Influencer). Remember, the boss is a big-picture kind of person. If the Conceptualizer gives his boss too much information, the boss's mind will wander. So what should the Conceptualizer do to satisfy his personal need for quality and accuracy yet still respect his boss's needs?

Perhaps he should tell his boss the three main points of the issue. He could then hand him a one-page point paper with the key issues followed by an appendix of the "gory" details (just in case the boss has trouble sleeping at night). Don't you think that would satisfy the boss's information needs? Stretching his style will promote a better working relationship for the Conceptualizer.

Now consider another example. A Driver (who has read *The Churchill Factors*) is dealing with a customer who is a Supporter. Who is faster paced? The Driver. Who takes more risks? The Driver. Who can work better in a changing environment? The Driver. For the Driver to deal with the Supporter, he must stretch out of his style to that of the Supporter. Thus, he must slow down the pace of his voice to that of the Supporter. He must also be warmer and more relational than he normally is. "How's the family? Don't you have a son in college?" The Driver should not throw change at the Supporter or ask the Supporter to deal with processes that may have some risk.

If we reverse the previous example, and the Supporter has read *The Churchill Factors*, the opposite situation applies. In this case, the Supporter has to speak at a faster pace than he may be comfortable using. Admittedly, it may be a greater stretch for the Supporter to speed up than it is for the Driver to slow down!

Anytime a person stretches outside his behavioral comfort zone, he will experience some stress and discomfort. The first time someone attempts to stretch, it will seem alien. The tenth time will be easier. Eventually it will become a conditioned response. People with any one of the four styles can, over time, master the technique.

Implicit in the previous examples is the need to be able to determine the behavioral style of the other person. One way is to learn the characteristics of all four styles and thus be able to recognize them in other people. Determining another person's style is called people-reading. There are techniques to do this, either in person or over the telephone. Appendix III will tell you how to obtain learning instruments and tools, such as People-Reading Cards and Action Planners, that will amplify these techniques. There are also several applications for managing performance, customer service, and sales.

One way to get a better appreciation of the four styles is to see the world through the eyes of others. What kind of information do they prefer, detailed or big picture? How do they deal with change and risk? Are they mission oriented or people oriented? Are they fast paced or more reserve paced? The four sections in *The Churchill Factors* can give you a glimpse of the different worlds.

Any time you desire to communicate more clearly, you will want to stretch out of your personal comfort zone. Since you have regular interactions with your boss, an associate, an employee, a customer, a supplier, a family member, a friend, and even a stranger, you may need to stretch often. Communication really counts!

In today's marketplace, people in organizations are asked to do more with less. Communicating effectively becomes the critical tool. Here's the progression of what must happen in order for an organization to communicate effectively. People must be able to establish rapport. Rapport opens the channel for communications and allows relationships to be established. When relationships are based on understanding and valuing the other person, trust develops. Trust promotes openness and even better communications.

> *"Every step we take—no matter how small—to understand the needs of the people we strive to serve will increase our bond with them and move us in the direction of a higher standard of leadership."*
> **Mahatma Gandhi**

People who cooperate and do not compete are then able to combine their individual talents, experiences, and knowledge to create new possibilities. Acting upon these new possibilities will enable the organization to move to that next level of performance. Imbedded throughout this whole process are vision, courage, and determination. Yet clear communications is the channel that lets new ideas and actions flow.

APPENDIX II

Favorite Books By and About Winston Churchill

Over the past three decades I have shared my interest in Winston Churchill with family, friends, co-workers, clients, and attendees at my presentations, speeches, and seminars. At a regional Churchill convention in Richmond, Virginia, in 1990, speaker and historian David McCullough (like many others before and since), asked my wife and me the question, "What is the single best book about Churchill?"

It's a good question without a simple answer. There are some two thousand books about the British statesman! They run the spectrum from Isaiah Berlin's short biographical sketch to Sir Martin Gilbert's official biography with eight volumes and fourteen companion volumes of correspondence (with seven more expected).

Over the years I have found myself going back to certain books over and over again. I would have to classify these as my favorites. I will provide short sketches of these books, both by and about Churchill. There are many other Churchill books that look at every facet of his life in great detail. The ones I have included, however, will get you started.

A number of the books are out of print. At the end I will tell you where you might be able to find these books.

BOOKS BY WINSTON CHURCHILL

Books by Winston Churchill will fill an entire bookcase, unless you happen to have copies of each of his different editions. In that case they would fill an entire room! Fortunately for new generations, many of Churchill's out-of-print books have been reprinted. **Richard Langworth's** *A Connoisseur's Guide to the Books of Sir Winston Churchill* (Brassey's, 1998) is the best reference to all the books written by Churchill. (Many times the title of Churchill's books in the U.S. is different from the title in Britain. When you look for his books, use the British title.)

My Early Life (*A Roving Commission* - U.S.), 1930.
Churchill's autobiography covering his youth, his school years, his military service in Cuba, India, Sudan, and South Africa (including his POW escape), and his early years in Parliament. Extremely entertaining.

Thoughts and Adventures (*Amid These Storms* - U.S.), 1932.

Churchill's thoughts on a number of different subjects: hobbies, painting, his spy story, anarchists, some experiences in World War I, and thoughts on the future.

Painting As A Pastime, 1948.

This small book was originally two chapters in *Thoughts and Adventures*. Churchill's discussion of life, stress, hobbies, books, and painting makes this one of his most charming and personal books. The wisdom between the covers is invaluable!

The Second World War, six volumes, 1948-1953.
Memoirs of the Second World War, 1 vol. abridged, 1959.

Churchill's perspective on the war starting with the roots of the conflict to the end of the war. Churchill had a front-row seat as Prime Minister from 1940-1945.

A History of the English Speaking Peoples, 4 volumes, 1956-58.

Covers the saga of English-speaking history from the invasion of England by Julius Caesar to Victorian Britain. There are several abridged one-volume versions including *The Island Race*, *The American Civil War*, *Heroes of History*, and *The Great Republic* (everything Churchill wrote about America compiled by Churchill's grandson **Winston Churchill**, Random House, 1999).

The World Crisis, six volumes, 1923-1931.
The World Crisis, one volume abridged edition, 1931.
　　Churchill's perspective on World War I, seen from his role as First Lord of the Admiralty, a battalion commander on Western Front, Minister of Munitions, and Secretary of State for Air & War.

Great Contemporaries, 1937.
　　Biographical sketches of several great historical figures including Baden-Powell (of Boy Scout fame), Lawrence of Arabia, George Bernard Shaw, Hitler, Trotsky, FDR, and others.

The River War, two volumes, 1899.
The River War, one volume abridged edition, 1902.
　　Describes the history of the British involvement in the Sudan. Churchill took part in the last great cavalry charge against the sword-whirling Dervishes. Even at an early age, Churchill's writing was powerful. The original two-volume work was beautifully illustrated with drawings and maps.

Savrola, 1900.
　　Churchill's only novel gives an interesting foreshadowing of his future career as a charismatic leader. A young and inexperienced Churchill displayed a remarkable understanding of politics, democracy, and statesmanship.

Blood, Toil, Tears, and Sweat: The Speeches of Winston Churchill, compiled by **David Cannadine**
(Houghton Mifflin Co., 1989)

There are many different editions of Churchill's speeches. This modern single volume has a selection of his best speeches from 1901-1955. Included are the most famous of his World War II speeches and his 1946 "Iron Curtain" speech in Fulton, Missouri.

BOOKS ABOUT WINSTON CHURCHILL

Churchill: Speaker of the Century (Stein and Day, 1980)
The Wit & Wisdom of Winston Churchill (Harper Collins, 1994)
James C. Humes

Churchill: Speaker of the Century may be the single most entertaining book about Churchill. Humes, a Presidential speechwriter, author, and humorist, frequently portrays Churchill. The book has enough charm to satisfy the casual reader and enough detail to satisfy the serious reader. Humes also has another book called, *The Wit & Wisdom of Winston Churchill,* an enjoyable compilation of Churchill's quotations and quips. Regrettably, both books are out of print.

The Last Lion: Visions of Glory 1874-1932 (Little, Brown and Co., 1983)
The Last Lion: Alone 1932-1940 (Little, Brown and Co., 1988)
William Manchester

For the person who likes history replete with drama and details, these are the most readable biographies about Churchill. Manchester's lordly writing style gives a Churchillesque account of Churchill's life. Manchester is adept at giving the reader the context of the times, which helps us understand the reasons why Churchill made his decisions. It is unfortunate that Manchester will probably not complete the third volume of this extraordinary biography.

Churchill: A Life (Henry Holt and Company, 1991)
In Search of Churchill: A Historian's Journey (Harper
    Collins Publishers, 1994)
A Photographic Portrait (Houghton Mifflin Co., 1988)
Sir Martin Gilbert

Sir Martin took over the job as official biographer of Winston Churchill after Churchill's son, Randolph, who began the monumental project, died in 1968. The eight-volume work is a scholarly, extremely detailed effort. He then condensed his eight-volume biography into the one volume *Churchill: A Life*. The result has more color and movement with less of the ponderous details of the official biography. It was ironic that Sir Martin never met Churchill (Manchester did), but he probably knows more about him than any other man living. His *In Search of Churchill: A Historian's Journey* is an extremely interesting and readable account of his meticulous efforts to know Churchill and bring him to the public's eye. *A Photographic Portrait* (Houghton Mifflin Co., 1988) is an excellent photographic biography of Churchill's life.

(It is estimated that over 30,000 photos of Churchill were taken during his long career!)

Clementine Churchill (Cassell, 1979)
Winston Churchill: His Life as a Painter (Houghton Mifflin Co., 1990)
Family Album (Houghton Mifflin Co., 1982)
Winston and Clementine: The Personal Letters of the Churchills (Houghton Mifflin Co., 1999)

Mary Soames

Lady Soames is youngest and only surviving child of Winston and Clementine Churchill. Her books are as vivacious and fascinating as she is. Her biography of her mother, *Clementine Churchill*, reveals a poignant dimension of Churchill's life. In a similar way, her biography of her father, *Winston Churchill: His Life as a Painter*, contains anecdotes and insights that only a family member would know. Her *Family Album* is a wonderful selection of family photographs with comprehensive explanations. Lady Churchill recently released, *Winston and Clementine: The Personal Letters of the Churchills*, that reveals much about the personal lives, interests, and concerns of her parents.

Churchill, Wanted Dead or Alive (Carroll & Graf Publishers, 1999)
The Young Churchill: The Early Years of Winston Churchill (Carroll & Graf Publishers, 1995)

Celia Sandys

Ms. Sandys is the granddaughter of Winston Churchill. Her books provide an in-depth examination of

Churchill's early life including his famous escape from the Boer prisoner-of-war camp and his school experiences. Both contain many photos and facsimiles of Churchill's letters.

Churchill's Last Years (David McKay Co., 1965)
Roy Howells

There are many books by the people who surrounded Churchill: his friends, his private secretaries, his physician, his bodyguard, his naval aide, his gardener, his research assistants, and the like. Here his medical attendant for the last seven years of his life gives a poignant recounting of Churchill. I particularly enjoyed the chapters on the foods Churchill liked or disliked and the ones about his pets. More formal biographies rarely dwell on such historically unimportant trivia, but they reveal yet another colorful side to the great man.

National Geographic, August, 1965.
Special coverage honoring Winston Churchill

W.S.C. A Cartoon Biography, complied by **Fred Urquhart** (Cassell, 1955).

Churchill: His Paintings, compiled by **David Coombs** (World Publishing Co., 1967).

Winston Churchill: An Illustrated Biography, by **R. G. Grant** (Gallery Books, 1989)

The four works listed above give a visual image of the real Man of the Century in photographs, cartoons, and oil paintings.

The Paladin, by **Brian Garfield** (Simon & Schuster, 1979)
The Proteus Operation, by **James P. Hogan** (Bantam Books, 1985)
Triumph, by **Ben Bova** (Tom Doherty Associates, 1993)
To the Honor of the Fleet, by **Robert H. Pilpel** (Atheneum, 1979)

Churchill's extensive involvement in the British government made him the subject of several fictional works. Some of the better ones are listed here. Pilpel also wrote **Churchill in America** (Harcourt Brace Jovanovich, 1976) an excellent non-fiction work about Churchill's fifteen visits to the United States. Many times the novelists stretched the truth about Churchill's actual involvement. While Churchill is not the main character in any of these works, the authors creatively inserted him into the plots. All four books make entertaining reading.

AUDIOTAPES OF WINSTON CHURCHILL

Winston S. Churchill: His Memoirs and Speeches
Twelve two-sided audiocassettes of Churchill reading some of his books and speeches. Several live performances are included. Originally from Decca LP's.

Books On Tape, Inc.
Over 5,000 full-length audiobooks read by professional voices. Many of the readers are British, and some affect a Churchillian accent for Churchill's words! Extremely entertaining. Books by Churchill include: *The Second World War* (6 volumes), *The World Crisis*

(abridged), *History of the English-Speaking Peoples* (4 volumes), *My Early Life*, *The River War* (abridged), *Great Contemporaries*, *Marlborough* (abridged), *The Story of the Malakand Field Force*, *London to Ladysmith Via Pretoria*, *My African Journey*, and several others by and about Churchill (including Martin Gilbert's one-volume biography of Churchill and William Manchester's two-volume biography). Contact Books On Tape at www.booksontape.com or 800-626-3333.

VIDEOTAPES OF WINSTON CHURCHILL

The Complete Churchill, 4 videos, A & E Home Videos (1-800-423-1212), 1992.

There are dozens of video documentaries about Winston Churchill. This is one of the best. Martin Gilbert, official biographer of Churchill, hosts this 3-hour documentary. Extremely comprehensive visual history particularly of Churchill's leadership while Prime Minister. It is unfortunate that Jack LeVein's twenty-six-part documentary, *The Valiant Years* (with music by Richard Rogers and Churchill's words spoken by Richard Burton), is not available on videotape.

WHERE TO FIND BOOKS ABOUT WINSTON CHURCHILL

New Books and Current Reprints of Books:
Churchill Center Book Service, **603-746-4433**
www.winstonchurchill.org (click "New Books").

The Churchill Center and the International Churchill Societies put out an outstanding quarterly journal called *Finest Hour* that contains articles about every facet of Churchill's life. There are many photographs, cartoons, and illustrations of Churchill. In addition, they have articles about Churchill on stamps and coins, memorabilia, book reviews, book collections, and Center events (seminars, conferences, and tours). Their web site contains a great deal of information on Churchill's speeches and writing as well as audio and video clips.

Out of Print Books:
Churchillbooks, **603-746-5606**
E-mail: rml@churchillbooks.com

Everything from autographed first editions of books by Churchill to inexpensive, reading copies of books by and about Churchill. This is the finest selection of Churchill books for sale in the world.

APPENDIX III

Learning Resource Center

PAINTING KEYNOTE SPEECH

I have developed a visual synopsis of ***The Churchill Factors: Creating Your Finest Hour.*** The painting keynote speech is called, ***Make Every Day Your Masterpiece.*** During the fifty-five-minute presentation, I complete a 36-inch by 24-inch oil painting to illustrate the compelling message of Churchill's simple formula for success. By combining this unique visual approach (including several visual surprises) with a strong suspenseful speech, the keynote reveals Churchill's best practices involving leadership and his proven strategies for success.

Like Churchill, the audience will learn how to:

- **Achieve heroic results**
- **Harness relentless resolve**
- **Turn adversity into advantage**

Executives, employees, and spouses will see and hear valuable lessons learned from one of the greatest leaders and motivators of all time.

Contact Homeport Training & Development to schedule the painting keynote or experiential seminars for your group.

Call toll free 1-866-KEYNOTE (539-6683)
Fax: toll free 1-877-353-8060
E-mail: HomeportTD@juno.com

EXPERIENTIAL SEMINARS

Inscape Publishing (formerly Carlson Learning Company) invented the learning instrument industry in 1972. Not only do their products set the standard for the industry, but their continuous improvement and continuous innovation have developed user-friendly tools for success. Their learning instruments allow a person or team to discover his strengths and then to develop strategies to use those strengths.

My seminars, workshops, retreats, and executive coaching programs use Inscape learning instruments. As an authorized Inscape distributor and certified trainer, I have found that people are able to remember, apply, and benefit from information that is experiential as well as intellectual in nature. My programs are customized (that is, tailored to specific client needs and expectations) and interactive. Each seminar gives participants immediate and specific feedback, techniques, and strategies for enhancing both personal and team effectiveness. Unlike other programs where the training seems to fade out not long after the event, my experiential programs are designed to produce memorable and lasting results.

Homeport Training & Development is committed to giving people and organizations the tools to be more successful. Corporations, government, associations, and educational organizations have benefited from the different programs we offer. Some of the most popular programs are:

- *Building An Unstoppable Team*
- *Creating Workplace Harmony & Cooperation*
- *Critical Communications*
- *Exceeding Your Customers' Expectations*
- *Selling With Style*
- *Selling For Non-Sales People*
- *Extraordinary Leaders—Extraordinary Results*
- *SOS: Stamp Out Stress (Executive Stress Mgmt)*
- *Making Time Work For You (Time Mastery)*
- *Supervise With Success*

These programs are available in half-day, full-day, and multi-day formats and are customized by combining learning modules from the different programs to meet the client's specific and unique needs. An underlying theme of all of the programs is that the learning must be practical, inspiring, timely, and fun. If you are interested in any of these programs, please call for additional information.

LEARNING INSTRUMENTS

Many readers will want to obtain copies of the learning instruments in order to optimize the information contained in *The Churchill Factors*. These learning instruments (also called profiles) and related tools may be purchased in special learning packages. The Inscape learning instruments contain understandable instructions to help an individual self-administer, self-score, and self-interpret the results. These tools are easy to use and easy to apply. There are personal action plans and strategies for success in each profile. The following are brief descriptions of the learning instruments and tools.

Instrument Descriptions

Focus Point™: Build rapport, trust, and openness in understanding self and others concerning behavior and communication. This profile goes into much greater depth about the four behavioral styles discussed in this book, and there are several levels of interpretation. This profile can be applied to change and transition, teamwork, mergers and acquisitions, coaching and mentoring, sales and customer service, and other applications. 27 pages.

Dimensions of Leadership Profile™: Discover the leadership potential at all levels of an organization and create active followership. Gives leaders an expanded menu of different leadership approaches for different situations. Learn why people follow, who will follow, when to lead, and what to watch out for when taking the lead. 19 pages.

Time Mastery Profile™: We mentioned briefly how important time management was in creating your finest hour. Develop or refine skills to set priorities, achieve goals, increase productivity, meet deadlines, control interruptions, enhance time teamwork, master paperwork, conquer procrastination, and other applications. 33 pages.

Innovate with C.A.R.E. Profile®: People prefer to innovate in one of four ways—creator, advancer, refiner, or executor. Learn how to achieve high performance teams based on team members' personal innovative strengths. Take teamwork and problem solving to the next level. 15 pages.

Coping With Stress Profile®: Learn how to develop proven and effective stress coping skills to enhance productivity at home and work as well as to achieve greater professional and personal satisfaction. 31 pages.

Discovering Diversity Profile®: Learn how to build a new understanding of others in a non-threatening way and how to make diversity a strength. 13 pages.

Personal Listening Profile®: Help people match and develop proven listening skills and approaches to their different communications needs. (Few, if any, people learn how to listen in school.) 15 pages.

DiSC® Relationship Profile: A guided process to help two people communicate more effectively and openly. Contains many strategies to ease conflicts, reduce misunderstandings, and increase mutual satisfaction. Couples married over 30 years have discovered ways to relate to each other better. 15 pages.

DiSC® People-Reading Card
DiSC®Talk (Telephone People-Reading Card)
Laminated, easy-to-use guides for mastering the art of people-reading in person or on the telephone. By identifying a person's style, know his motivations, greatest needs, greatest fears, decision process, behavior under pressure, and more.

DiSC® Talk Action Planner
DiSC™ Management Action Planner
DiSC™ Customer Service Action Planner
DiSC™ Sales Action Planner

These action planners help in stretching out of a behavioral comfort zone and being on the same communications "center frequency" as others. There are specific strategies for applying the DiSC technology to managing and coaching employees; being more responsive to customers, bosses, peers, and employees; and selling to people with different behavioral styles.

Instrument Packages

The four Training Packs are designed to give you the tools to discover your people strengths and then to develop strategies to apply these strengths. The Vision, Courage, and Determination Training Packs build on the technology you covered in *The Churchill Factors*. The Finest Hour Training Pack helps you reach that next level of personal and professional development.

Vision Training Pack: $29.95*

1 copy of **Focus Point**™
1 copy of **DiSC® People-Reading Card**
1 copy of **DiSC®Talk (Telephone People-Reading Card)**
1 copy of **DiSC® Talk Action Planner**

The Vision Training Pack helps you to discover your specific behavioral style. **Focus Point**™ gives detailed information about each of the four behavioral styles as well as descriptions of the different combinations of the four styles. The people-reading cards help you to determine another person's principal behavioral style either in person or on the telephone.

Courage Training Pack: $46.95*

1 copy of **Focus Point™**
1 copy of **DiSC® People-Reading Card**
1 copy of **DiSC®Talk (Telephone People-Reading Card)**
1 copy of **DiSC® Talk Action Planner**
1 copy of **DiSC™ Management Action Planner**
1 copy of **DiSC™ Customer Service Action Planner**
1 copy of **DiSC™ Sales Action Planner**

The Courage Training Pack gives you the contents of the Vision Training Pack plus three action planners that teach you how to stretch your behavioral style to adapt to the other person. You will receive specific information for relating to management, sales, and customer service scenarios.

Determination Training Pack: $76.95*

1 copy of **Focus Point**™
1 copy of **DiSC® People-Reading Card**
1 copy of **DiSC®Talk (Telephone People-Reading Card)**
1 copy of **DiSC® Talk Action Planner**
1 copy of **DiSC™ Management Action Planner**
1 copy of **DiSC™ Customer Service Action Planner**
1 copy of **DiSC™ Sales Action Planner**
1 copy of **Dimensions of Leadership Profile**™
1 copy of **Time Mastery Profile**™

The Determination Training Pack gives you the contents of the Vision and Courage Training Packs plus one copy each of a powerful leadership profile and a time management profile. These two profiles give you specific techniques for enhancing your personal leadership and management style. Leadership and time mastery are two of the most important keys to success for any organization or profession.

Finest Hour Training Pack:　　$73.95*

1 copy of **Innovate with C.A.R.E. Profile**®
1 copy of **Coping With Stress Profile**®
1 copy of **Discovering Diversity Profile**®
1 copy of **Personal Listening Profile**®
1 copy of **DiSC**® **Relationship Profile**

The Finest Hour Training Pack gives you five profiles designed to enhance your people skills. You'll learn specific techniques for applying your innovative talents, dealing with stress, working with a diverse work force, improving your listening skills, and developing stronger relationships.

FREE 30 minutes of telephone consultation offered with the purchase of any of the Training Packs.

---

*Call for shipping costs and sales tax.

Acknowledgements

Not long ago someone asked me how long it had taken to complete an oil painting that I had made. I smiled and replied, "All of my past life has been but a preparation for this effort." So it was for writing *The Churchill Factors: Creating Your Finest Hour*.

"Writing a book is an adventure. To begin with it is a toy, an amusement; then it becomes a mistress, and then a master and then a tyrant. And just before you are reconciled to your fate, you slay the dragon and cast it upon an unsuspecting public."
Winston Churchill

I have been blessed by the contributions of many generous, knowledgeable, and conscientious friends. Some contributed countless hours while others offered a word of encouragement at just the right moment. Without their dedicated help, this book would not be possible.

Special thanks is reserved for Duvall Hecht, Jim Auer, Jim Davidson, Jess Brasher, Richard Langworth, Dave Gulitus, Paul Stanley, Jack Womack, Bill Robinson, Wanda Beersdorf, Ron Cohen, Jess Foltz, Wyman Howard, Susie Moncur (at Inscape Publishing), Debbie Romero (at Action Printing), and the entire team at Trafford Publishing.

My entire extended family (the Kryskes, Gottliebs, and Moreheads) was greatly loving, supportive and encouraging. I especially appreciate the help from my dad and from my son, Paul K. I also want to recognize two men whose love, friendship, and encouragement made a difference in my life: my late fathers-in-law Bud Morehead and Charlie Hedigan.

I would be remiss if I didn't single out my wife, Naomi, for work above and beyond the call of duty. Awesome would best describe her involvement in every facet of the book. Her contributions to this book were so significant that her name ought to be on the by-line. Regrettably, I will honor her request not to call this a joint effort. My love for her remains unbounded.

The Lord has blessed me in so many ways, and all praise, glory, and honor rightfully belong to Him!

"... but united, concentrated, combined, working together in true comradeship, there is no foe who can bar our path."
Winston Churchill

Postscript

Congratulations on completing this book! The baton has been passed to you! *The Churchill Factors* gives you a simple formula for success. It's simple to understand, but it will also require your discipline and dedication. You must be willing to apply the techniques described in the book. You must be open to the new possibilities that you will experience on your journey toward your finest hour.

"The price of greatness is responsibility."
Winston Churchill

Never forget that you were created to be a masterpiece. You possess all the innate talents to lead a joyful, productive, successful life. *The Churchill Factors* will give you a proven way to make your dreams come true. It is my hope that you will experience a richer, fuller, more purposeful life. I look forward to hearing from you about your success stories. Live victoriously!

Homeport Training & Development
Quick Order Form

☎ Telephone orders: Toll Free 1-866-539-6683
    Fax orders: Toll Free 1-877-353-8060
💻 E-mail orders: HomeportTD@juno.com

Please send the following:

❏ *The Churchill Factors*   ____ copies @ $17.95
❏ Vision Training Pack   ____ copies @ $29.95
❏ Courage Training Pack   ____ copies @ $46.95
❏ Determination Training Pack ____ copies @ $76.95
❏ Finest Hour Training Pack   ____ copies @ $73.95
❏ Other _____
❏ Information about seminars & workshops
❏ Information about painting keynote speeches

Name: _____

Business: _____

Address: _____

_____

City: _____ State: ____ Zip: _____

Telephone: _____

E-mail: _____

Homeport Training & Development
Quick Order Form

☎ **Telephone orders:**   Toll Free 1-866-539-6683
   Fax orders: Toll Free 1-877-353-8060
💻 **E-mail orders:**   HomeportTD@juno.com

Please send the following:
❑ *The Churchill Factors* _____ copies @ $17.95
❑ Vision Training Pack _____ copies @ $29.95
❑ Courage Training Pack _____ copies @ $46.95
❑ Determination Training Pack _____ copies @ $76.95
❑ Finest Hour Training Pack _____ copies @ $73.95
❑ Other _____
❑ Information about seminars & workshops
❑ Information about painting keynote speeches

Name: _____

Business: _____

Address: _____

_____

City: _____ State: _____ Zip: _____

Telephone: _____

E-mail: _____

ISBN 155212459-2

9 781552 124598